C000254718

A YEAK Uɬɬ

HOW TO TAKE A GAP YEAR AND TRAVEL THE WORLD EVEN IF YOU ARE ON A BUDGET

In 25 Easy-to-Follow Steps

By Maggie M. Gómez

The Nomadelle® LLC Publisher

Copyright © 2020-2021 by Maggie M. Gomez

Published by The Nomadelle® Co.
The Nomadelle® Co. is a registered trademark of Fly Me More LLC
210 Gilman Ave
Cincinnati, Ohio 45219 USA

Library of Congress Cataloging-in-Publication Data
Gomez, Maggie M.
A Year Off: How to Take a Gap Year and Travel the World Even if You Are on a Budget
Maggie M. Gomez
Library of Congress Control Number: 2020905768 (English)
Library of Congress Control Number: 2020905766 (Spanish)

ISBN: 978-1-7347370-0-4 Paperback (English)
ISBN: 978-1-7347370-2-8 eBook (English)
ISBN: 978-1-7347370-1-1 Paperback (Spanish)
ISBN: 978-1-7347370-3-5 eBook (Spanish)

Printed in the United States of America

Cover by Youness El Hindami
Book layout design and formatting by Saqib Arshad
Photograph of Author by Flashback Foto Cincy

All referenced books and the The Creative Platform digital course contain affiliate links in the digital format of this book.

To my family and my true friends, especially my 'Champeteras'.

This book is dedicated to Gary Vaynerchuk. He doesn't know who I am, but his daily inspiration and perspective taught me to love myself and to seek happiness above anything else. I didn't know how to do any of that before.

TESTIMONIALS

"*A Year Off* by Maggie Gomez is extremely well written! I have always loved traveling and immersing with people in their fascinating lives and cultures. It has been a long time dream to travel the world, experience the beauty of diversity, exchange positive vibes with wonderful people, and breath in the fantastic landscape.s with which we have been so blessed. Prior to reading this book, I didn't believe that I had the time or financial resources to pursue these goals. The author has inspired me to focus on solutions, not obstacles [...] Following these simple steps, we can achieve goals that seemed insurmountable."

- Steve Dunham

"I love your book! Although world travel isn't a priority for me, it still captures a philosophy I've had for a long time: discover what you love doing, then figure out how to get paid for doing it. If your book had come across my eyeballs years ago, I might be a world traveled musician by now! [..] But the book is laid out methodically and you keep the reader interested with your writing style."

- Rich Stuhler Jr.

"[This] is a persuasive publication that has made me rethink the prospect of travelling abroad. Through her words, Maggie allowed herself be vulnerable; and in-turn my mental barriers were lowered, allowing me to receive her guidance with arms wide open. Her passion and compassion bleed through the pages, reassuring that world travel is not just for the well-off. After reading this book, I feel like I'm a part of a community of travelers where knowledge is shared, hearts are opened and dreams are achieved."

- Teddy Jagielski

"Thank you for blessing me with your writing. It's inspiring. I have been talking about pursuing my passion so much lately. Your book is just confirmation."

- David Johnson.

"*A Year Off* is a simple step-by-step transformational guide for anyone that has dreamed of or thought about how to travel full-time on a budget and still make money. Maggie does an excellent job of drawing inspiration from her life, travel, educational and career experiences to develop a common-sense approach that contains lots of simple checklists, self-directed exercises and tips. If you can dream of traveling the world on a budget, then you can choose to accomplish it. All the decision and action steps are listed in the book! Everyone should read just to understand what's possible when you find your passion and decide to act on it."

- Calvin Decker

"This is a very well written book with tons of practical information. Whether you, like the author, are planning to take a year off work, or are thinking about pulling up roots and moving or are looking for basic financial planning information, this will be a great resource. I highly recommend it!"

- Joe Pearce.

Table of Contents

Table of Contents [Cont'd]

A LETTER FROM ONE NOMAD TO ANOTHER

If you're reading this, you may have always had a desire to travel the world, but something probably triggered you to take the action to transform your life now. Our journeys are probably very different from each other's, but at the end of the day, we are all people looking for happiness. The fact that you bought this book is a proactive step toward a transformation, and it tells me that you are finally ready. Welcome to the beginning of your new life as you've always dreamed it.

As I write this intro, I'm weeks away from getting on a plane to Santiago, Chile, where I'll start my year-long adventures throughout South and Central America. If someone would have told me a year and a half ago that this was going to happen, I would not have believed it for a second. But here I am, finalizing my packing list with all the things I'll take with me to the trip of a lifetime. Hopefully, the first one of many.

In fact, my life was quite different not too long ago. Up until March of 2018, I had worked for one of the largest financial companies in the US for 11 years and was the happiest employee on the face of the earth, until one day, I was laid off. I couldn't find a job that I liked as much as my financial job and

I was unemployed for several months. By then, I had taken antidepressants for 15 years, but without a job and no health insurance I had to stop taking them overnight. I went on a downward spiral at the same time that I was offered a job at a company that I knew was not right for me. However, I could not bring myself to wear a suit, go job hunting, and put on an interview face, so I most graciously accepted the job that was offered to me and I started selling telecommunication infrastructure. I hid my depression and anxiety very well.

A few months later, I hit rock bottom. It was very difficult for me to get out of bed - I could hardly move, I could not eat or sleep. I hate guns but own one for self-defense. One night I got up and walked toward the place I kept it because I decided that I could no longer take the pain. I had lost the most satisfying job that I've ever had, my heart had been recently bruised, I hated my current job, my mother had just been diagnosed with Alzheimer's, I had recently fallen out with a close family member, and the chemical intake provided by antidepressants which had once kept me going, stopped abruptly. All that in a matter of months. I was sobbing uncontrollably as I was walking towards the gun. On one hand, I was anticipating the relief of the unbearable pain I had been feeling for so long and that I could no longer take. But on the other hand, I was devastated by the thought that I was not going to be able to experience things that I hoped to one day experience.

As those thoughts ran through my mind and as I was getting closer to the gun, I screamed, "Enough is enough!" I told myself that I must find a reason to stay; I can't give up. I always wanted to travel the world and even though I couldn't afford it at that moment, I was going to make that my only mission in life. I remember that night very vividly. It was April 30th of 2019. I gave myself 365 days to figure out a way to start traveling the world, whatever it took, because that is what I always dreamed of doing. It was the same night that I promised myself to never ever consider anything but life and happiness. And in the crazy event that the plan worked, as a way to pay it forward and to give back to the karma gods, I was going to share the steps I took with whoever needed it as badly as I did. I walked away from the gun and little by little, I started to embrace a bit of myself each day by working hard to figure out how to afford traveling the world with my almost non-existent budget.

Something in me changed when I made the conscious decision to follow my dream and to do what I always wanted to do regardless of the million reasons I shouldn't. Things started to become clearer and I no longer felt anxious or depressed. I guess that when you are true to yourself and to others, all fears dissipate, and you feel strong in a way you have never felt before. Even if things didn't work out, I said to myself, I knew that I could find a job easily after my year off (or six months, or whatever), as employers nowadays value more and more an employee's exposure to world travel. Not that I ever want to go back to a 9-5, but in the case that things wouldn't go as planned, there was still a way out, as I always have an exit strategy up my sleeve. I knew at that moment that everything was going to be alright.

All and all, I've done a fair share of traveling in my lifetime but had never taken an extended period (of more than a month) to really dive into travel like some people have been able to do. I've always wanted to take a gap year and travel the world full-time, but I never thought that this was possible because I assumed that it required me to be rich. During my research I learned that this assumption couldn't have been further from the truth and discovered that many people travel full time with a very limited budget. I had to find a way to travel economically and to make money while on the road. I experimented with a few different projects. Some failed and some succeeded. My biggest takeaway, which is also the common message from everyone in the same boat is: find something you feel passionate about and monetize that. If you monetize on an activity that you do not feel passionate about, things will get difficult fairly quickly.

However, I had no idea what my passion was in life, besides traveling. I always felt that everybody was good at something except me. I never felt like I could figure out what my calling was. It took a lot of time, soul-searching and retrospect to understand that the answer was always in front of me. I've always been drawn to understanding what makes cultures similar and different from one another. It started when my family and I moved to Venezuela due to a civil war in our hometown of Chile, and we became political refugees. Even though I was little, I became aware that people spoke differently and behaved differently than me. I was so drawn to those differences and very badly wanted to understand why it was that way. Not only that, but I was also fortunate enough to be able to attend an international school in Caracas, the Emil Friedman musical school. There, most kids came from different countries and cultures. As a result of this experience, my love for understanding cultural differences and similarities from a psychological perspective was born. It never left my side, even though it took decades to reclaim this passion and make it my life mission.

Now I just had to figure out what the full-time travelers meant by 'monetizing' their trade. They call themselves 'digital nomads' and I wasn't sure exactly what that meant, but I knew I wanted to be one. For a whole year, I didn't stop reading books about this, watching videos, listening to audio books, talking to a lot of travelers - all with the goal to understand the many ways to afford traveling without being rich and while on a budget. In a few sections of this book lies the summaries of my findings explained in a way that's scalable for anyone to follow and replicate.

There have been so many ups and downs throughout the year leading to my departure. For each moment that I thought I had it, there were ten instances when I felt that I had failed and was not going to be able to take the time off as I had planned. Based on that, I should have quit a trizillion times but never did; I kept on going. Retrospectively, it was probably all those daily motivational Gary "Vee" Vaynerchuk videos that prevented me from quitting. This is why I'm dedicating this book to him. Eventually, everything worked out and my flight is scheduled for May 1, 2020. Exactly 365 days after I made that promise to myself. It's crazy how things work out. Please do not give up. Ever. No matter what. This is a marathon, not a sprint, like Gary always says. If you fall, figure out why and start again. It does not matter how many times you have to start again. I believe in you. Start believing in yourself.

I will soon embark in an unforgettable adventure and will go from country to country, observing cultures, taking pictures, posting on social media, interviewing locals, and speaking to teens at schools about the importance of learning about cultures. I will soon be living life to the fullest like I've never done before. Only now I understand how fragile and transient life is. Part of me wonders why I didn't do this sooner but part of me also understands that I probably wasn't ready. Always remember, you are one decision away from a completely different life. Your time is now. Find your passion, pack your bags, and go.

I wish you the best on your journey. May your internal shine never be tamed again.

Happy travels!

maggie m. gomez

AUTHOR

When was the Last Time You Took Inventory of What Truly Makes You Happy?

The first edition of this book contained a post scriptum that explained my timeline a bit better (see last page). You're reading a revised first edition, not quite a second edition. In a nutshell, here's what happened: I spent a year planning my nomadic life, but a month before I was scheduled to travel all borders closed due to the Coronavirus. I spent another year in quarantine like everyone else and now I'm finally ready to venture into the world of solo travel. Well, sorta. I have not received the COVID vaccine, not my turn yet, but I'm only going to visit my family in Chile for a couple of months. I'll then assess where I'll go after that. Maybe I'll come back to the

States to get my vaccination so I can travel with a little bit more freedom. We'll see where the wind blows and I may follow.

However, as I start getting ready for my second attempt to travel, and in a very creepy deja-vu sort of way, an interesting thought has invaded every one of my brain cells as of late. Much before the beginning of the global outbreak, I was determined to put happiness in the priority of the list of things that drove the direction of my life. Once the global pandemic took over our lives and everything started to close down, we were all confined to the isolation of our homes and there wasn't much that any of us could do about it. That's when many of us started to question our sanity and, as a result, our daily habits. If, at some point, we ever wondered why we followed a routine that we loathed, in a structured 8-6 schedule that sucked our lives away, surrounded in an environment that didn't make us thrive, well, after the Corona-triggered social isolation we sure knew then that we had the ability to stop the routine. Any routine. This was a powerful discovery. A discovery that we didn't have before, ever since the industrial revolution gradually silenced our brains and obligated us into a structured way of living in exchange for a sense of security called 'paycheck' with the only condition that our dreams were not ever to be unmuted.

Once we were confined to work remotely or do things differently than what we have done before because of COVID, for the first time in our lives, we witnessed that a pattern could be broken, the world continued turning, and yet we were still breathing. This is incredibly significant from a psychological perspective because it is the first time that we have proof that we can break the mold and things can still be okay. Things were (and are) not the same, by any stretch of the imagination, but we can manage and we can adapt. See, before social isolation started, we yearned for things to be different but lacked the courage to change them fearing the unknown. We were more terrified of the consequences of what we did not know. Should we be the responsible party to change the routine of life's sustainability? But, we were not the ones who broke the pattern. The pattern was broken because of an external situation (Covid-19) which caused us to stay home in order to survive. We witnessed that we *could* change our lives, that we *can* question things, that we *can* take inventory of what truly makes us happy and act upon it. At minimum, we can draw a plan of action and follow it. Now we know it is possible to break free, to grow wings, and to fly.

I've been glued to social media for the past year thanks to the mandated social distancing, and I have witnessed incredible talent, dreams, passions, desires to learn, to be better, to do the right thing, and to help others. If this quarantine has taught us anything at all, please let that be about how short of a span life has. Literally. Please do yourself a favor and go live your life the way you want to live it. How? I don't know, figure it out. Use this book as a starting point. There is no time to waste!

"I always wondered why birds stay in the same place when they can fly anywhere on this planet. I thought about this for a while and then I asked myself the same question." -HY

INSTRUCTIONS

These are literally the 25 steps I took from the time I decided to turn my life around and take a year off from the 9-5. But this is not intended to be a year-long vacation. In fact, it's far from it. I haven't worked so much and so hard in my life as I have now, but I do it with love and joy because I'm doing it for me and not for anyone else. I've never felt this way about myself before and it feels great. I wish the same for you, and here's a summary of what's going to happen as a result of your perseverance towards taking the steps outlined in this book: you're going to work hard to discover what your passion is (unless you already know what it is), you're going to work hard and find a way to monetize on it while on the road, and you're going to learn the not-so-glamorous aspects of planning a gap year that nobody talks about. I will be here with you all the way through.

If you thought that this was going to be your year off to do nothing while sipping margaritas on a tropical beach, this is not the right book for you. IF you're ready to work your butt off for a year (or for however long you'll set up your timeline to start your best life yet) I'm proud of you. You have my 100% guarantee that your life will be so incredibly different from one year to the next. This will be the beginning of your best self yet.

The steps I outline are in chronological order... somewhat. There will be times when one of the tasks will be ongoing and you will have to start the next step before you finish the previous one. For example, the first step is to start listing all aspects of your life. As you go through the next steps, something will trigger you to think of more items to add to that list, and so on, and so you may revisit that step again. Do this at your own pace and always do what's right for you. Possibly, you may have to do some steps sooner than what's outlined here. This is completely fine. I'm just sharing what I did merely as guidelines for you to do what makes the most sense for you.

These are the three main areas of focus of this book: finding what makes you happy, learning how to afford a year off, and sabbatical planning. Each step contains not only the information you need, but also my personal perspective as I went through it, and an assignment or task to help you stay on track. I've also added a timeline, but this is a rather subjective time frame since we all have different realities and different priorities. Take mental notes of what works for you and what doesn't. Take actual notes if you think of additional steps not included here that might work better for you. In fact, what helped me tremendously was to use a notebook and write down everything I thought I needed to accomplish. In a way, you are reading a polished and organized version of it. Alternatively, a journal-version of the notebook I used is also available if needed. You can purchase this through the same source where you purchased this book.

Lastly, since my trigger was my strong desire to come out of a place of darkness, I devoured as many self-help and business books as I could. I will share with you the titles that impacted me the most and which influenced the way in which

2

I built my journey, one way or another. I feel that I got a second chance in life and this is my way to paying it forward. I truly hope that it serves you well. Whether you choose to read them (or to listen to them like I did, for the sake of time efficiency) or not, that's completely up to you and even though I think they will enrich you tremendously, I don't think that not reading them will negatively affect the results of you following this book's recommendations.

Before taking Step 1, please take a selfie - no filter - and in whichever mood you are currently: sad, angry, happy, anxious; whatever triggered you to pick up this book, capture it. Right before you take off on your gap year, take another selfie. Compare both. You'll be amazed at how the difference in your internal energy makes your face look so different.

Again, this book is just a guideline to help you take the action you need to turn your dreams into reality and to be the author of your own life. This is what worked for me, but you do you. Ready to transform your life? Start by reading The Right Mindset.

THE RIGHT MINDSET

Before we dive into all the excitement of planning to travel the world and explore your passions, it's important to take a slightly deeper dive into assessing your motivations for travel, as well as your overall mental health. Do you want to travel because you are severely unhappy at home and are convinced that this is the only way for you to find happiness? If so, you might need to re-evaluate your mindset before beginning to travel, as this can set you up for higher expectations than may be able to be met.

I am not going to lie, what brought me to wanting to travel the world was the worst depressive episode I've ever had. It was very scary. Taking my mind off of it by planning a trip of this magnitude worked. In fact, I listened to an audio book that helped me more than anything else has ever had to get over the generalized sense of depression that I never thought I could overcome. This depression had many causes and deep roots from my childhood, but that's a story for another book. Nowadays, not only am I off antidepressants, but I also live a happy life despite its imperfections. The name of the book I listened to is called *Lost Connections* by Johan Hari. After reading it, I quickly understood that taking a trip to run from myself was not going be a sustainable solution. Instead, I've learned to love myself in ways I didn't realize were possible before. Today, I write this book from a place of contentment and happiness, knowing that it is possible to train your mind to do whatever you want.

Here's a summary of the most important points I learned through this and other similar books: There's a concept frequently discussed in psychology called the abundance mindset, which is in direct opposition to the scarcity mindset. These mindsets both fall in line with the concept of self-fulfilling prophecy, which is the idea that whatever you tell yourself will eventually become true. If you keep telling yourself that you will never be happy until you travel the world, you will continue to be an unhappy person in your own environment. However, if you shift your mindset to telling yourself, "I can be happy right where I am. Joy can be found in the here and now," you will start to believe this to be true and eventually find happiness exactly where you are. How does this relate to abundance and scarcity mindset? Scarcity mindset is when you look around your environment and notice all that is lacking for you. You might see someone that is traveling the world on social media and think, "I'm never going to get to do that; they're so lucky. I have no money to be able to do what they can do." You are focusing on all that is missing from your world, and you will continue to draw that negative energy toward yourself and continue to find yourself lacking. Abundance mindset, on the other hand, is shifting your mindset to believing that you have more than enough available to you. The thoughts shift to looking like, "There are plenty of travel opportunities available for me. Money will continue to flow in such that I will be able to afford exactly the type of travel that I desire." I'm not saying you'll win the lottery tomorrow (but maybe that's some scarcity mindset creeping in!), but by shifting your attitude, you will draw more opportunities to you that align with the thoughts and feelings you're projecting into the world.

I know this mindset shift sounds easy; however, it takes a decent amount of practice and dedication to get used to catching your thoughts and reframing them in a way that better serves you. First, you have to become aware of your thoughts and what messages you are telling yourself. You can do this by doing a "mind dump," which is where you write down all of the thoughts that are flowing through your mind for about 5 minutes and go back and examine what you've been telling yourself. You can also do this by paying attention to moments in the day when you're feeling particularly joyful or negative and see what you were just thinking about right before that. Did you see photos of someone traveling on social media? Were you able to catch what thoughts came to mind in that moment? Record those thoughts so that you can be aware of the specific messages that come up for you.

Once you have an awareness of the thoughts, you'll want to engage in thought stopping and redirecting. Once you notice the thought, tell yourself "stop," or "be quiet," or whatever works for you, and redirect your thoughts in a more positive direction. If the message was, "I'll never have enough money to travel," stop yourself and redirect to something more adaptive, such as, "I am continuing to pull in enough resources for what I need. I have a plan to help me achieve my goals. Everything is as it should be." The more you do this, the more you will begin to notice your energy shifting in a more positive direction and the more you'll realize the positivity you're pulling into yourself. Even if this sounds too "woo-woo" for you (it did to me when I first heard of this), do me a favor and try it for 30 days. I would love to hear what changes this brought to you.

If you find you're having a hard time doing this, or the negative/scarcity thoughts are more than you can handle, consider attending a mindfulness group or visiting a therapist to work on assessing and changing the thoughts. Having accountability and others alongside you in the process can be very encouraging and helpful for creating change.

Now that you've started working on your frame of mind, we can begin the exciting work of digging in and discovering your passions! The next few steps are going to help you consider what it is that you love to do and allow you to narrow down your options, and this new frame of mind is going to help that process entirely.

SET UP A TIME FRAME

If you are anything like me, you know that if you wait until you have everything figured out in order to set up a timeline, you might never set one up. Knowing that I'm a perfectionist and that I can't move forward if my current task is not completed to perfection, what worked for me was to learn to just take a leap of faith, and thus, I set up a timeline of 365 days where I was supposed to: come out of the financial hole I was in, save money to travel, figure out a plan that would allow me to be financially self-sufficient while traveling, put all of my affairs in order, and figure out all the details that come with planning a gap year. That time pressure is very valuable because setting a time frame in spite of not having anything figured out is optimal and is quite alright. Setting a time frame of when you want to leave will provide the end goal that will allow you to manage your resources and your time most effectively. It will give you the pressure you need to be as creative as you possibly can in coming up with ideas and ways to make your dreams a reality. Depending on your situation, 365 days might be a good estimate. This will give you time to draw a plan of action and execute to the best of your abilities in a very efficient manner.

Although you are creating a timeline to keep things on track, be flexible to know that your timeline might be a moving target depending on how well or how quickly you are able to complete all 25 steps outlined below. Be mindful of your bad habits and allow yourself to learn from past mistakes and improve your processes to bring the most efficient self in you. I personally had many of these bad habits. The first time to start working on them is hard, but like anything else that you practice - you get better at it and develop to the point of liberation. For the sake of illustrating an example, I'm just going to point out how crippling my perfectionism has been. In one of the sections in Step 8 (Step Up Your Money Game), I talk about starting a YouTube channel because it could be quite a profitable endeavor if you do it right. My very first video took almost a year to create and upload because everything had to be perfect, the stars had to align, and the constellations in the universe had to give me the right type of sign. Knowing this weakness of mine allowed me to improve in that area, to be less of a perfectionist, and to just do it. If I waited for the right time and the right skills to make my first YouTube video, I could have been waiting forever. Not only should this journey be an opportunity to create the trip of your lifetime but let the preparation for it be the time that you need to fall in love with yourself by forgiving your past mistakes, strengthening your mental and physical capacity, and improving - even if a tiny fraction - anything about yourself that hinders your ability to be sincerely happy.

So, what's your timeline? When do you want to take that initial flight towards the first day of the rest of your most fulfilling life yet? Well, it will heavily depend on your current circumstances. I, personally, was able to pull it off within a year but I probably could have done it in six months if I had a book like this one guiding me through. However, if you need to take longer than six months or a year, good for you for understanding where you are. You're in this for the long run. Be kind to yourself and take care of whatever you need to take care of first. I'll still be here supporting you every single step of the way.

AUDIO/BOOK RECOMMENDATION: One audio book that tremendously helped me overcome the feeling of being overwhelmed by the task at hand was Unfu*k Yourself by Gary John Bishop. Please check it out if you have a moment. It helped me put everything in perspective and become much more purposeful and effective in my thoughts and actions.

THE 25 STEPS

A Timeline

Anybody, regardless of their age, can take a year off their 9-5, even if on a budget, if they plan it well. To be fair, and to qualify this further, I should add that anybody **with a computer** and **basic computer skills** can take a year off by following the steps outlined in this book. In this age of technology, money resides in the digital world. It does not matter whether you are 20, 30, 40, 50, or 60 years old. You have to adapt to the way the world flows and that's through a virtual prism. You can put your life on hold for a year all you want. Heck, upon your return you might find a better job than the one you left behind simply because employers nowadays value world and cultural exposure now more than ever before. Alternatively, you may find that this nomadic lifestyle suits you better and want to prolong your journey indefinitely. But in order to sustain yourself on the road, you have to figure out ways to monetize your knowledge, your skills, your adventures, your learnings, your humor, your perspective, or anything that people are willing to pay for in the way of digital real estate. You need to become a **digital nomad** and we'll talk about how to do that in a minute. Making and selling t-shirts is fun, but it's not a feasible way to support yourself when traveling unless you leave someone you trust to manage the business for you. Believe me, I tried, but nobody is going to care about your business as much as you do. This is probably one of the hardest lessons I learned when converting my plan into actionable steps. Instead, always assume that this project is a party of one (unless you have a partner to share this journey with), create your own specialty based on what you love, get good at it, learn it, teach it, spread your passion, touch lives, create amazing content that people will want to consume because you love it and you feel strongly about it.

It took me a while to understand what I loved so much that I wanted to share it with the world. But when I did, I felt like I could move water upwards and no longer cared about any internal or external mental blocks that I had ingrained in my mind over time. Up until that point, I was very shy and terrified of criticism. I never posted anything personal on social media because I thought that nothing of what I had to say had any value. But when I found my creative genius, there was no stopping me. This book is a reflection of what happened after that realization.

What follows is a sample of what my timeline looked like. In retrospect, I wish I had a visual aid like this one when I started my journey. It would have made things so much easier, and it would have saved me half the time I wasted in figuring things out. Not to mention, it would have saved me a lot of money I spent experimenting with a few business ideas. Though I appreciate the lessons of the downs as much as the joys of the ups, I don't want you to go through the hassles and pains I did, and I don't want you to make the mistakes I made. Instead, I choose to share this timeline with you as a way to give back to the universe and to make your journey much easier. But don't forget that this is still YOUR journey. If you need to modify things, please do so. If you need to change things around, by all means do. If you know it will take you longer than 12 months, who cares, go at your own pace but don't stop moving.

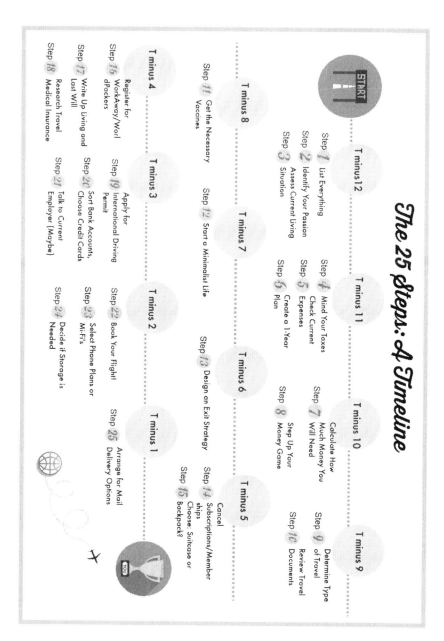

The 25 Steps: A Timeline

START

T minus 12
- Step 1 List Everything
- Step 2 Identify Your Passion
- Step 3 Assess Current Living Situation

T minus 11
- Step 4 Mind Your Taxes
- Step 5 Check Current Expenses
- Step 6 Create a 1-Year Plan

T minus 10
- Step 7 Calculate How Much Money You Will Need
- Step 8 Step Up Your Money Game

T minus 9
- Step 9 Determine Type of Travel
- Step 10 Review Travel Documents

T minus 8
- Step 11 Get the Necessary Vaccines

T minus 7
- Step 12 Start a Minimalist Life

T minus 6
- Step 13 Design an Exit Strategy

T minus 5
- Step 14 Cancel Subscriptions/Memberships
- Step 15 Choose: Suitcase or Backpack?

T minus 4
- Step 16 Register for WorkAway/World Packers

T minus 3
- Step 17 Apply for International Driving Permit

T minus 2
- Step 18 Sort Bank Accounts, Choose Credit Cards
- Step 19 Select Phone Plans or MiFi's
- Step 20 Book Your Flight!

T minus 1
- Step 21 Arrange for Mail Delivery Options

- Step 18 Research Travel Medical Insurance
- Step 17 Write Up Living and Last Will
- Step 24 Decide if Storage is Needed
- Step 23 Talk to Current Employer (Maybe)

Table 1

Note: This timeline reflects my journey and, therefore, is set up as 12 months (hence, T -minus 12), as that was my target timeframe. Adjust accordingly if you need to increase or decrease the unit of measure.

16

WHAT IS A DIGITAL NOMAD AND HOW DO YOU BECOME ONE?

It took me a long time to understand this, but I finally did. By no means do I believe I cracked the code quite yet. In fact, I just started and that's why it's easy for me to convey that anybody (with a laptop and basic computer skills) can take a gap year or longer to travel the world, even while on a budget. This book is about the practical steps to get you there, but the following diagram best reflects the options that you have in finding a way to support your travels for a year (or longer):

How to Afford a Gap Year

OPTIONS:		UPFRONT WORK*	WORK DURING TRIP*	POTENTIAL EARNINGS WHILE TRAVELING:
Option A:	Save Enough Money to Afford a Year Off	4 of 5	0 of 5	None
Option B:	Work Virtually or Teach Locals (i.e.English)	1 of 5	3 of 5	Up to what employers offer
Option C:	Create a Digital Shop	5 of 5	3 of 5	The sky is the limit

* Degree of Effort: 0 = None   1 = Light   2 = Some   3 = Moderate   4 = A Lot   5 = Excessive at Times

Table 2

18

To reference the chart above, under Option A, you can work extra hard right now and save enough money to take a gap year and not have to worry about much more while traveling. Technically, if you combine it with free room and board (more on that on Step 9), you only need money for airfare, local transportation, travel medical insurance, and emergencies. That's all. Ideas on how to increase your savings and earnings are listed on Step 8.

Working virtually for someone else or as a freelancer, Option B, allows you to have some income as you travel, but usually just enough to get by. That is not to say that some freelancers make a pretty good living while on the road. Should you choose to do freelance work, you'll be limited by the work that you are able to receive. Also, should you choose to work remotely, hired by someone else, your funds will be limited to what your employers pay you. You can also teach English (or anything you're good at) wherever you decide to go. The upside here is that if you stay in one place long enough, you could also learn the local language, which makes you a lot more marketable. Step 8 will provide several links to places looking for remote employees, or freelancers. There is a lot to choose from, depending on your skills, certifications, and experience.

Creating a digital shop, Option C, is the path that's going to take the most work on your part both upfront and during your trip. However, the potential earnings are so incredibly high that, in my eyes, any amount of work is worth it. This is the path I took (as well as half of Option A). I'm sharing my lessons in this book so that you can avoid the mistakes I made and succeed in your search for freedom from the rat race. There are many things that you can do to create your digital shop and

Step 8, as well as the 'Elements of a Digital Shop' section right after it, detail important aspects to consider. However, in order for this digital shop to be sustainable and to work successfully, it has to be based on what you consider to be your life passion (or passion<u>s</u>). Step 2 will help you understand why it is so pivotal and necessary to identify what makes you happy and to incorporate that into your digital shop. For now, here's a diagram that helps explain how it's all twined together.

Option C: Create a Digital Shop

(Your Passion + World Travel = Endless Content) + Your Offering = Source of Income

PROS:

If built correctly, there is no cap to the earnings and stream of income that your shop could generate

You will be building your own personal brand

Your time abroad will be mostly spent on your passion, as it becomes the topic of your trip

CONS:

Setting up your digital shop is a lot of work

Depending on the offering(s) that you create, as well as the upkeep, you might have to work hard (at least initially) while traveling

Table 3

To put it simply, a "digital nomad" is the person who uses technology such as a laptop or a camera to earn a living. This gives people the freedom to work from anywhere and it makes it very attractive for those who wish to travel the world. You don't have to be an expert to get started - I wasn't. In fact, nobody starts as an expert, but getting started and being consistent is the key to succeeding. Even if you suck at the beginning (we all do), practice makes perfect. You can proudly call yourself a "digital nomad" should you choose either option B or C.

HOW TO BECOME A DIGITAL NOMAD

The Big Picture

#1 MOST IMPORTANT
- Travel the world, discover yourself
- Be happy!
- Help others

#2 NEXT STEPS
- Find your life passion: This becomes the focus of your trip
- Determine how your message (your focus) can help or inspire others
- Understand **why** you feel passionate about your topic and **why** you want to help others through your message

#3 BUT BEFORE YOU START TRAVELING...

- **Create an offering that will generate revenue**
  Examples: an online course, coaching, digital services

- **Place your offering on a digital platform**
  Examples: Facebook, YouTube, your website

- **Publish regular content, which reflects the message that your want to convey based on your target audience. Your awesome content attracts traffic to your offering.**
  Examples: as a blog on your website, as a post on social media, as a vlog on YouTube

- **Run ads to direct traffic to your digital platform or where your offering can be found**
  Examples: through Facebook Ads, or Google Ads Sense

Table 4

In order to become a digital nomad, it's important to understand the big picture. Let's look at the three aspects that highlight the life of a digital nomad running a digital shop, per the image above:

#1 Most Important: Of course, we all want to travel the world and discover things. As long as we treat others the way we want to be treated, our only goal in this life should be: to be happy doing what we love and help others do the same.

#2 Next Steps: Here's where you should start giving your trip a specific purpose. In my particular case, my passions are cultural differences from a psychological perspective, traditional ethnic dances, and creating manuals. Therefore, I travel the world interviewing locals in order to understand why people in that specific geographical area behave the way they do. I participate in as many traditional dances as I can either by learning them or by documenting them. Lastly, I write the steps I take to accomplish a goal so that it's scalable if I want to do it again, or just to perfect the process. I've done this my whole life, especially in corporate, every time I started a new role. I was known for writing manuals and policies and procedures, and I believe this skill contributed to the rapid progression of my career when I used to work the 9-5. Detailing steps so that no one else had to reinvent the wheel was my bread and butter. Ask any of my past employers or previous managers and they'll all reference my educational materials. So, those are my angles. What are yours?

#3 But Before You Start Traveling: After identifying what I felt passionate about and what I loved doing, I started narrowing down my niche and my target audience. It was time to start creating content that was interesting and that I had fun developing. After all, if there is something that you love so much, you should explore it and share it, even if nobody pays attention. However, for the sake of financially supporting your travels for an extended period of time, let's try to generate enough quality content to grow a fan base. There are a huge number of ways to do that. I only point out the few that I've tried myself. I'm in the process of developing a digital course. I finally got the courage to create a YouTube channel, and I'm being more consistent in posting blogs on my website. All of these efforts, along with Facebook Ads or Google Ads, drive the traffic needed for people to become aware of what I have to offer. This is now starting to generate the funds that will sustain me during my travels. Again, I'm a regular person, just like you. If I was able to do it, you can too!

Always remember that if you think you don't have what it takes to post content regularly or to create videos for a vlog, just know that we've all felt that way when we first started. Keep an open mind - everything else is learnable. Think of an amateur video that you may have watched recently that has inspired you to take some sort of action, whether it was on YouTube, Facebook, TikTok or anywhere else. Just like their video, your content, raw and unpolished as it might be at the beginning, could also touch someone else's life. Above all, think of the level of happiness that you'll feel as you work hard every day to follow your dreams by creating that content just because you believe in it.

STEP 1

Make a List of Everything. Everything!

In a notebook exclusive for this project (or in the journal companion), start making a list of all aspects of your life. This will be particularly helpful to avoid anything falling into the cracks and to ensure that you have everything under control as you plan your gap year. The purpose of this exhaustive list is to identify everything that at one point or another will need to be addressed and assessed. If you think that this is an overwhelming exercise, you're correct. First, it proves how many unnecessary things that you're tied to. Second, it allows you to minimize the things that you will worry about while on the road. Third, it will allow you to place them in their own sub-categories so that you can address them and create a plan of action to achieve your goal by your specified timeline.

Examples of items in the list could be your car, house, health insurance, computer, phone, bank accounts, etc. First, go through each room and just write down what you see. Don't ever stop adding to this list and get as granular as you need to get. Eventually, this list will give you three things (1) it will identify the material things that you will have to either sell, donate, give away, throw away, leave as is, replace, or store. This list will also (2) allow you to identify those aspects that will have to be planned around for your actual trip such as photography equipment, storage, prescription medicine. And lastly, (3) this list will provide a list of items that you can cut off with the purpose to eliminate costs (i.e. cable), lower costs (i.e. phone plan), or negotiate a better deal (i.e. credit card interest rates).

Main List and Sub-Lists

Sub-Lists

Main List (Brain Dump)

(1) **Money-Related** (You will need this on Step 5)
a. Cut off
b. Lower cost or negotiate

(2) **Start a Minimalistic Life** (You will need this on Step 12)
a. Sell
b. Donate (ask for a tax receipt)
c. Give away or throw away
d. Leave as is
e. Replace
f. Store

(3) **Subscriptions & Memberships** (You will need this on Step 14)
a. Eliminate
b. Suspend
c. Maintain

(4) **Trip-Related** (You will need this on Step 15)
a. Bring (packing list)
b. Buy
c. Don't lose sight

Table 5

If it helps, here's a small sample of my own list(s) but you can break it down in whichever way makes sense to you:

(1) Money-Related
   a. Cut off:
      i. Netflix
      ii. Cable
      iii. Weekly movies at the movie theatre
   b. Lower costs or negotiate:
      i. Credit card interest
      ii. Better phone plan

(2) Start a Minimalistic Life
   a. Sell
      i. Bookshelf
      ii. Tent
      iii. Laser printer
   b. Donate
      i. Clothes, shoes, purses
      ii. Furniture
   c. Give away or throw away
      i. Speakers
      ii. Collection of recipes
   d. Leave as is
      i. Most my furniture (since I rented my house out furnished)
   e. Replace
      i. Range stove
      ii. Shower curtains
   f. Store
      i. Bike
      ii. Paintings
      iii. Collection books

(3) Subscriptions & Memberships
   a. Eliminate

i. Netflix
  ii. CBS All Access
b. Suspend
  i. Phone carrier
c. Maintain
  i. Graphic design platforms

(4) Trip-Related
  a. Bring (packing list)
    i. Camera
    ii. Tripod
    iii. Clothes
  b. Buy
    i. Good raincoat
    ii. Sheet liner
  c. Don't lose sight
    i. Prescription medicine
    ii. Passport

From this point forward, and as you add items to your list, you should be aiming to reduce clutter as well. Step 12 (Start a Minimalistic Life) will address this aspect in more detail, but the truth is that it's never too early to start a minimalistic life, especially in preparation of your year off. The more you can get rid of early on, the better.

AUDIO/BOOK RECOMMENDATION: I can't think of a better way to kick things off than recommending one of my favorite audiobooks, *High Performance Habits* by Brendon Burchard. It gets me energized every time and I feel very productive after listening to each chapter. It starts off with a self-evaluation, which you have to repeat once more after you finish reading the book. This allows you to compare your trajectory of improvement, which is pretty impressive.

TASK 1.1

Create your main list and never stop adding to it. From there, create your four sub-lists, which you will need in subsequent steps: (1) Money-Related, (2) Start a Minimalistic Life, (3) Subscriptions & Memberships, and (4) Trip-Related. It is okay for an item to be in more than one sub-list. Any version of this is absolutely fine as we all have our own system of categorizing and structuring things.

STEP 2

Identify Your Passion

You, like most of us on this planet, have a passion for traveling and discovering places that you've never been to or heard of before, or even know how to pronounce. Unless you have the means to take a year off and vacation anywhere you please, you have to find a way to bring meaning to your trip. There are two reasons why it is important for you to do that: (1) because life is so much better knowing what you're good at and doing what you love; and (2) we'll utilize that passion, hobby, or skill to monetize on while on the road, which is what will help you support your travels and will give an even deeper meaning to them. So, what makes you unique and different from anyone else? What is that one life passion that you have that brings joy to your soul and body? But more importantly, what is it that you want to get out of your year of travel?

For most of us, these are not easy questions to answer. We have been conditioned all of our lives to not do what we want to do, but rather, do what pays the bills. So now, how do we even start identifying the things that make us happy if we've had to repress them most of our adult lives?

I had the most difficult time with this task. Mostly because I never felt that I was good at any one thing in particular except for the financial job I held for years. When I lost that, I felt that I had lost my identity. I always felt mediocre at most things and, on many occasions, I simply tried to find something that would just generate money. Having this mentality causes us to stagnate growth. When we focus on the money (or lack thereof) and not on our true passion (what is abundant within ourselves that we want to share with the world) is when we attract scarcity. In fact, when I started taking a deep dive, observing, and listing all the things that put a smile on my face without any effort, that's when I finally realized what gets me going and I'm naturally good at. I was able to realize that I love cultures because I like to understand what makes them unique and what makes them similar to one another. Traditional dancing is one of these aspects, and I decided that I wanted to start documenting the different dances of all the countries I visited and create videos about it. I wanted to do this, selfishly, because I did not want to forget the beauty of what I was learning as I travelled the world, but also because I was hopeful that one of those videos could inspire someone to learn more about the cultures of the world and, therefore, be more tolerant of one another as humanity. That is what I wanted to get out of my trip - that was my entire mission, to convey the message that learning about cultures makes us better humans. When I started to focus on the true love for my passion, that's when things finally started to be clearer and started to fall into place from an abundance perspective. I was no longer chasing dollar bills. Instead, I was attracting what I loved about life and giving it my own personal spin. Huge difference.

A client of mine, who has been a dental hygienist all of her life and still loves it, is in the process of creating a digital course which she will use to teach rural villages from Central and South America how to acquire better dental hygiene habits in order to improve their lives. That is what she will focus on when she starts her journey. I have another client who has not yet been able to find her life passion. And that's okay. It is not an easy task and sometimes it takes a lifetime to discover what you love. We must not dismiss that for some, a passion is a constant search. For instance, some may want to rely on their love for volunteering as their mission for their travel. That's absolutely fine and there is nothing wrong with that. However, if that's you, I would always recommend keeping your mind, eyes, and ears peeled in case you come across something that fills your heart. When you do, explore it to the max, be patient, give it time, and give it lots of love.

Unless you already know what your passion is, write down things that you enjoy doing, even if they are simple. Go back in time and remember what made you happy, what made you smile when you were a kid, a teenager, a younger adult. Identify a pattern, group them together, and start thinking about ways that they could be integrated in your travels. Imagine how the different countries and cultures could influence the way that you could explore those passions. In other words, make the world your never-ending canvas where you can paint your story using any colors you like, drawing the objects of your attention, all that captures your heart and your creative genius.

Identify your top passion and also a secondary passion, if possible. Let's look at the reasons why this is important. A passion:

- Brings you happiness
- Teaches you the importance of self-care
- Gives you a reason to keep learning and to improve on something specific
- Provides you with a topic during your travels, something to focus on
- Gives you a great excuse to experience something new in a new place
- Brings you together with others who share the same interest

This is your chance to explore what makes you absolutely happy. Know that whatever you come up with will likely be the focus of your travels. Based on what we'll cover in this book, your passion will also be the source of monetization down the road. Make sure that you choose something that you love doing or learning about. Here are a few ideas to inspire you:

What Inspires You?

Animals	Fruits
Art	Hats
Arts & Crafts	Health
Astronomy	History
Buildings	Museums
Children Books	Music
Colors	Ocean
Community	Photography
Cooking	Planes
Cultures	Plants
Dancing	Teaching
Eco-Farming	Tourism
Exercise	Trains
Extinct Animals	Unicorns
Farming	Volunteer Work
Fashion	Water Sports
Food	Yoga

Table 6

Until we get to Step 8 and learn the practical ways to put our passions to work for us, there are a couple of things that you can do in the meantime. Research, read, do what you can to try to become an expert on them, the go-to person. It doesn't mean that you have to be one right now but aspire to do so. This is probably going to be a stretch for most (it definitely was for me) but start building a social media presence around your topic. This will allow you to feel more comfortable communicating to others and sharing your experiences. Eventually, little by little, this will help you increase your fan base because later on, you'll see how the larger the fan base, the better chances of monetizing you'll have. Start posting daily on social media, or as often as you're able to, but be consistent. Choose one or two platforms at the beginning, such as Facebook and Instagram. Pictures or videos tend do better than written content as people are very visual. It sure does seem like our attention span is getting shorter and shorter each day. Pose a general question or statement about any of your topics. Be positive, teach, acknowledge what you've learned, thank people, and reference experts. Look at the influencers you admire and do something similar, but with your own twist. You'll see how this will help you increase engagement and possibly open the door for collaborations.

I personally went years without posting anything to Facebook because I used to despise social media. Also, I was a very private person and a serial introvert with major social anxiety. I never wanted anybody to know my business. When I started exploring social media as a way to connect with others who loved traveling and cultures as much as I did, my perspective about social media switched drastically. I was able to think of social media as a means to communicate with others using a common language. I still don't post much on my personal Facebook page, but I have a business Facebook page where I post very regularly. I interact daily with strangers on Instagram and Twitter who comment on my posts and I'm even able to answer questions on other people's posts. I'm able to provide a perspective that is unique because, well, because we all are. My goal is to get you thinking about what makes you unique, what perspective do you have that's different from the rest. It could be something funny, it could be something philosophical, or technical. Your goal is to figure out what it is that you must learn, know, and master if you would like to be known as the world expert on such and such. Focus on the answers and just do it. Use social media to learn, connect, and help.

AUDIO/BOOK RECOMMENDATION: This is a beautiful book that I never get tired of listening to. *The Art of Thinking Clearly* by Rolf Dobelli seems perfect right about now because it will help you identify the ways you think and transform your decision-making abilities. Understanding the simple errors that we make daily while building our train of thought will help you look deeper within and, along with this step's exercises, will help you explore the questions that will seek to understand what your life passions are.

TASK 2.1
Identify your top passion. Though optional, feel free to identify a secondary passion.

TASK 2.2

Understand the why behind your choices. Why did you choose this or that passion? The goal is to understand the true motivator, the true driver of your actions as that will be the constant reminder of the reason(s) you are doing what you're doing. There will be times where you'll be challenged, tired, exhausted and being clear on your motivation will help you overcome any obstacle that comes your way.

My personal example has to do with the various endeavors I attempted throughout the years. It was so much easier to give up and declare defeat when I was engaged in tasks not related to my passions. However, when I was able to identify those passions, giving up on the tasks related to them was not an option. If tasks were related to what I loved doing, I kept going despite any obstacles and challenges.

TASK 2.3

As you work on identifying those things that you feel passionate about, start thinking about who the people are that you are looking to have an impact on. This is called your niche audience. For example, most people could teach anything online. Just as an exercise, explore topics you think you could teach about and define your target audience. What's their age range, gender, other demographics? Any special needs? Start defining the type of individual(s) who you are most likely to create content for. Learn about your favorite topic, whatever inspires you, and create an outline about it with at least 10 different aspects about that topic. Play with the possibilities.

Bonus: What power adjectives describe you?

The first step on this journey to finding your passions begins with envisioning the best version of yourself. I don't mean the best version of yourself as you want others to see you, but rather how you want to see yourself, how you imagine the best version of yourself to look like. Having a clear vision of the end result is positive not only for your psyche as you move through this journey, but it allows you to create concrete actionable steps to take you to that place. It can be very difficult to accomplish a goal with an abstract picture in mind. Therefore, I'm going to help you get specific with your vision so that you can discover your passion and become the best version of yourself.

To start this process, review this list of the following 135 power adjectives. Look through each one and circle those that most align with your vision of the best version of yourself. To start, you can choose as many as you want, knowing that with time, you're eventually going to narrow that list down to only three adjectives. Why? Because it's important to be clear and specific so that these three words can be your mantra as you begin this adventure. Here is the list of the 135 power adjectives. I took this list from an article on

www.resumecompanion.com:

Which 3 Power Adjectives Will Define You?

• Accomplished	• Consistent	• Extensive	• Motivated	• Significant
• Accurate	• Constructive	• Fastidious	• Multifaceted	• Sincere
• Adaptable	• Controlled	• First-Class	• Novel	• Skilled
• Adept	• Cooperative	• Flexible	• Objective	• Skillful
• Advanced	• Cordial	• Fluent	• Orderly	• Smooth
• Agile	• Cost-effective	• Focused	• Passionate	• Sophisticated
• Alert	• Countless	• Genuine	• Perceptive	• Spirited
• Amiable	• Cutting-edge	• Groundbreaking	• Persistent	• Steadfast
• Amicable	• Dedicated	• Harmonious	• Personable	• Strategic
• Articulate	• Deep	• Honest	• Pleasant	• Strong
• Astute	• Dependable	• Ideal	• Positive	• Structured
• Attentive	• Detail-Oriented	• Imaginative	• Practical	• Studious
• Businesslike	• Determined	• Impartial	• Precise	• Superior
• Calculating	• Devoted	• Industrious	• Productive	• Sustainable
• Calm	• Diligent	• Influential	• Professional	• Systematic
• Capable	• Diplomatic	• Ingenious	• Proficient	• Team-Minded
• Charming	• Discerning	• Innovative	• Profitable	• Thorough
• Cheerful	• Discipline	• Insightful	• Progressive	• Thoughtful
• Clear	• Diverse	• Instrumental	• Punctual	• Timely
• Coherent	• Driven	• Intelligent	• Qualified	• Tireless
• Cohesive	• Earnest	• Inventive	• Quality	• Unique
• Committed	• Economical	• Investigative	• Resilient	• Unprecedented
• Competent	• Elegant	• Keen	• Resourceful	• Vast
• Complex	• Energetic	• Logical	• Respectful	• Vigorous
• Comprehensive	• Enterprising	• Loyal	• Revolutionary	• Well-Grounded
• Concerted	• Exact	• Methodical	• Robust	• Wholehearted
• Conscientious	• Expert	• Meticulous	• Shrewd	• World-Class

Table 7: *Source: www.resumecompanion.com/how-to-write-a-resume/resume-adjectives-guide/*

TASK 2.4

On the first page of your notebook, write down your three power adjectives. Read them out loud every day. Live by them and let them shape the way you now live your life, the way that you are now discovering the best you you've ever been. As you build your personal brand and as you start learning what your life passions are, these power adjectives will help you define who you want to be as you become an expert in your field.

As a way to explain the concept of 'personal branding', just think of the manner in which you present yourself to the world. Regardless whether you are promoting something or not, the way you speak, the way you interact with others, your demeanor, what you value, etc., all that forms part of your personal brand. Going forward, be mindful of what you express verbally and non-verbally. Work towards understanding what it's important to you as that is a reflection of your personal brand. These three power adjectives will remind you of what that intention is. Read them daily:

My 3 Power Adjectives

1

2

3

Task 2.4

STEP 3

Assess Your Current Living Situation

Your current living situation will be very impactful in the planning of your sabbatical year. Do you own or rent the house you live in? If you rent, your life just got a lot less complicated. Just make sure that you align your travel with when your lease ends. The timing of when to notify your landlord about your plans will depend on you. As a landlady myself for 10 years, I appreciate honesty and transparency over anything else. I always had a 30-day notice rule in place, but the sooner I knew of my tenants' plans, the sooner I could start arranging for a replacement for when the exit date came. Not all landlords are created equal, so be mindful of all the possible ways that your conversation with them could go. Above all, be respectful and if needed, explain that your plans are still up in the air and that you will keep them up to date on any progress. Also, inquire about the possibility of going month-to-month after the year lease ends in case that is needed.

If you're not renting, do you own a home? Are you better off selling it or renting it out? The best advice that I can give you regarding this topic is to speak with an accountant that can provide a high-level picture of your tax implications should you decide to sell versus to rent. If you're still paying a mortgage on your home, the pros of renting it out is the equity that you could build on it while away. Also, the security to come back to your own home should something go wrong, or any time for that matter, is priceless. The con of renting it out is that if you're still paying a mortgage on it, it will not likely be a significant source of income and you will need to pay property taxes and property insurance. If you own a home and it's paid off, I would strongly recommend that you rent it out, as that will provide a nice monthly income. The only caveat on that plan is that you will still need to pay for property taxes, and property insurance.

If you are still wanting to go the route of renting your home out, start shopping for property managers as soon as possible. When I started talking to property managers, I had them go through all the rooms of my home and point out everything that they thought I needed to fix to make it a desirable house for potential renters. I did that early on so that I could take care of what I needed without rushing. A 10% cut (plus a month's worth of rent) from property managers is a very standard rate. You can try to negotiate anything above that and bring it as close as 10% as you can. Property managers will find you tenants and they will collect the funds and deposit them into your bank account. If something breaks, such as your washer or dryer, they will replace it for you at an agreed upon cap. They'll deal with the tenants, which is ideal because you won't have to worry about any of those concerns while traveling. Ask them as many questions as possible and make sure to get in writing the answer to all of your questions. Review the contract and have another set of eyes look at it as well. Be inquisitive, yet transparent. Understanding expectations from both sides goes a long way.

As far as the property taxes go, try to pay a year in advance. Either way, go to the county clerk of the tax division of your city and find out schedules and ways to pay electronically while abroad. Explain what your plan is in case there are aspects that they recommend for you consider.

As far as property insurance goes, speak to your insurance agent and ask them if a BOP (Business Owner Policy) makes sense for you. This type of insurance combines building coverage and liability insurance, which is optimal, since you'll have tenants living in your house. Make sure that you get a copy in advance of the proposed coverage and premium and understand what is and what is not being covered. Ensure that you request all the possible discounts that apply to you. For example, if you have a security system in place, if you have fire extinguishers and fire alarms on all floors, if you pay your property insurance through direct deposit, etc., all of that is grounds for discounts. Additionally, your property manager will require renters' insurance from your tenants.

Whether you decide to sell or to rent out will depend on your personal situation. Besides deciding to take a year off, this will probably be one of the most important decisions that you'll make in the planning stage.

TASKS 3.1

IF <u>YOU RENT</u>: Write down a summary of your conversation(s) with your landlord. Put on your calendar any important dates such as 'last date to confirm 30-day notice', or 'notify landlord of any updates', etc.

IF YOU OWN AND <u>DECIDE TO SELL</u>: Write down important next steps and the conversations you have with everyone involved, as it will be easier for you to know where you are and where you left off. Put on your calendar everything you need to do or follow up on with your realtor, contractor (if applicable), bank agent, and accountant.

IF YOU OWN AND DECIDE <u>TO RENT OUT</u>: Write down important next steps and the conversations you have with everyone involved as it will be easier for you to know where you are and where you left off. Put on your calendar everything you need to do or follow up on with your property manager, contractor if applicable, tax clerk, and home insurance agent. Make sure that you add property taxes and property insurance to your list from Step 1, as well as in the appropriate sub-list(s).

STEP 4

Mind Your Taxes

Without exaggeration, I'd say the author that has had the most impact on my personal finances has been Robert Kiyosaki through his book *Rich Dad, Poor Dad*. Through his teachings, I learned the most underrated and valuable lessons that one could learn: What are assets and what are liabilities. Pretty much everything else in successful personal finance stems from these two concepts. Assets are things that you own and that can provide future economic benefits because of their potential to increase in value. Liabilities are things that depreciate and that will not replenish in value. Examples of assets are cash, investments (potentially), real estate property, etc. Examples of liabilities are car payments and most of the material things that you own and that will not hold value for long such as clothes and shoes. So, what's the name of the game? In a very simplified way: to amass far more assets than liabilities. In fact, aim to get rid of as many liabilities as you can so that the money that comes in is increasingly and exponentially higher than the money going out. It's not that liabilities are evil, but the fewer fruitless expenses, maintenance, and costs you have, the better and more simplified your life will be, which is just what you need when you travel.

Are you still trying to find the relationship between assets, liabilities, and this step's topic about taxes? Aside from the fact that Rich Dad, Poor Dad is the #1 personal finance book of all times and that it was written by the most famous accountant in the present time? Not much other than the fact that a good accountant will be able to look at your current finances, consider your travel plans and potential earnings, and advise you on the best moves to lower your tax liability to the lowest possible bracket. For example, once you start earning income from your travels (monetizing on YouTube as a content creator, as a freelancer, or as an English teacher) you may want to start recording all the expenses related to your travels for a possible tax deduction. Depending on your situation your accountant might advise you to create an LLC (Limited Liability Company) or file taxes as a Sole Proprietor. The idea is to protect your assets and minimize your tax liability. A good tax advisor or accountant can guide you in the right direction.

In fact, regardless of what time of the year it is, you should probably make an appointment with your accountant or tax advisor and share your plans to take a year off. There are many aspects that you should consider in order to be as prepared as possible for tax time. A tax advisor will be most suitable to look at your situation and tell you what you should consider in order to have the least impact possible on your taxes and therefore, the most positive impact on your finances. Find out how to manage the earnings that you will be making while traveling. Consider taking a course on bookkeeping or sending your accountant your balance sheet on a regular basis so that they can manage tax filing for you. Discuss all those details, as well as a way to sign digitally, in case you're out of the country when taxes are due.

If your tax advisor recommends that you itemize on your taxes, consider all of the donations that you will be making as you get rid of your material possessions. In fact, start thinking and planning about taxation all year round, not just when you have to file. Specifically, regarding donations, some would argue that they want to give without getting anything in return (altruism). Asking for a receipt from Goodwill, Salvation Army, etc. doesn't negate your decision to be altruistic. It simply allows you to be financially practical (and prevents the IRS from keeping more money than it should) while still giving to others who are in need of the items you have to donate. These are completely unrelated intentions and serves all of those involved. So, let's look at this in more detail. Contributions to qualified non-profit organizations may provide a tax deduction (only if you itemize). The way it works is that the amount that you contribute reduces your taxable income, which, as a result, decreases your deduction, which decreases the tax liability that you have to pay.

Now, let's put the above savings, along with all the possible savings you'll be working toward into perspective by applying the concept of compound interest. Let's say that by tracking all those contributions, and utilizing that tax deduction, you save $1,000 a year. This is probably a high number, but not unrealistic at all. For example, if you did that every year and you put that money into a low money-earning instrument that would allow for compound interest, such as a money market that pays 2% interest (rates may vary per state and financial institution), in 5 years, instead of having $5,000 dollars you will have $7,348, and in 10 years, you will have $14,355. Now tell me, do you still want to forgo those tax deductions? Go ahead and play with all the possible scenarios by using any compound interest calculator on the internet (I recommend using www.investor.gov).

By the way, do you know how compound interest works? It's not magic. It's just interest that keeps on calculating on an adjusted amount. Let's say that you have $100 stashed somewhere and take it to your bank. Your bank then will take your $100 along with everyone else's money and they will be able to invest these millions, thus earning interest. Of course, your bank will keep a portion of that interest but will share the rest of that interest created with all the people such as yourself who contributed to this big payday. So now, instead of $100, you now have $102 (assuming that your bank gives you a 2% interest). Your bank will do this over and over, and that interest will likely be calculated on a monthly basis. So why is that good? Well, that money will increase exponentially because the interest will be calculated not just on the principal amount but rather on the principal plus the interest earned, every single time. Pretty nifty, eh? Now you can see why wealthy people seem so rigid with their money. It's not because they became greedy (although that could be true for so many) but it's mostly because eventually one learns that every little bit helps and contributes to the increase of the principal. It's a snowball effect after that.

Interest on money markets are usually compounded daily and paid monthly. Sadly, the 2% interest mentioned above is pretty standard nowadays, but this percentage depends on so many factors such as the financial bank or institution that is offering the rates, the state you live in, or the instrument used as a vehicle to provide the compound interest. Examples of these instruments could be a money market or a CD (Certificate of Deposit). Before the 2008 recession, banks, CDs, money markets, etc., were able to provide up to 3.5 times the interest that they are able to provide now. But these same instruments were not yielding any interest for probably ten years after the real bubble burst and all went to shiest. So yes, even though it's low now, it's better than it's been in a very long time.

Lastly, all the interest earned, dividends, as well as any money that you may have made selling stock in the market is taxable. But please note that I'm specifically referring about non-retirement accounts here, and whether you withdraw or not the funds after you sell stock. If you held the stock for a year or longer after selling it, you incur in long term capital gains, which is a lot less than short term capitals gains. Ensure that you make your tax advisor aware of any market movement you may have made in order to see if there's any strategic move that could be done to offset your gains.

TASK 4.1

Make an appointment with an accountant or a tax advisor. Tell them about your plan to take a year off and, based on your current tax situation, find out how you should prepare or what you should consider in order to be ready for your next tax season. Document your conversation, as well as follow ups.

TASK 4.2

Make sure that tax planning is part of your main list from Step 1 and ensure it's added to the appropriate sub-list(s), if applicable.

Evaluate Your Current Expenses

You may have noticed that the title of this book references the possibility for you to take a gap year even if you are on a budget. I strongly believe that you should be able to travel because you are on a budget. Unfortunately, most people associate 'being on a budget' with a negative reality, with a lack of money perhaps. I strongly believe that the opposite is true and I'm here to attest that the sooner you adopt this way of thinking and start building a budget, the sooner you'll be able to buy that plane ticket that you've been dreaming of for so long.

Analyzing your current finances may be both eye-opening and heart-crushing at the same time, but as a result, you will start uncovering where you are from a budget perspective and where you need to be to start traveling and fulfilling your dreams. Even if you think you don't overspend and even if you have built a healthy savings, you will immensely benefit from doing this money exercise. This process will allow you to set the pace by which you will achieve your goals so that you can start creating your dream life and within the timeline that you have set for yourself. Planning is everything when it comes to accomplishing challenging tasks such as this one. Knowing what your assets are at the present moment (even if they are in the negative column of your personal bookkeeping ledger) and knowing where they need to be will help you organize yourself and set up goals to achieve your ultimate objective and live your best life yet, regardless of your age.

First things first. Ask yourself, who are you from a money perspective? If someone were to look at you and your current financial life, what would they say about you? How would they describe you? Let me give you a few examples, none of them are very glamorous:

- Man in his 20s with student loans, eats out every day.
- Woman in her 30s with 10K in credit card debt, renting an apartment, car loan, no savings.
- Man in his 40s, a mortgage, few credit card debts, some savings.
- Woman in her 50s, a mortgage, not sure about savings, spends a lot on shoes, car lease.

Now it's your turn… go ahead. No judgement, as this is just a way to objectively understand where you are today. Write one-sentence describing yourself financially right now. Forget the could have's, should have's, and all the would have's in your head. Let that be the last time that you beat yourself up about your past choices. Move on and don't dwell, but also take ownership and responsibility; more importantly, know that you now have the power to turn your life around. Once you've written your descriptive sentence, write down how you would want to be described instead, say, in a year from now. Dream big and write down what comes to your mind even if it sounds unrealistic. Now, work hard to become that person. Isn't it easier when you know what your goal is?

In a super generalized way, there are three facets of your personal finances that you will want to look at: bookkeeping, accounting, and investments. What's the difference between these three areas?

Think of **bookkeeping** as the individual entries in your bank statement. It's everything that comes in minus everything that goes out. It's the detail that reflects what you earn and what you spend on a daily basis. The goal is to eliminate as many of the entries of money going out as you can - but just those that do not contribute to the increase of your assets.

Next, think of **accounting** as a bigger picture, the one that will guide you through taxation based on your earnings and expenses. This is why you spoke to a tax advisor in Step 4. Also, accounting will look at the type of business entity that might be best suitable for you, should you ever decide to incorporate a business or your personal brand.

Lastly, **investment** is the way you strategically plan and allocate your net profits so that they grow (or maintain the inflation rate at minimum) and you can save more and earn more. Do you know to the penny what you have right this minute in your bank account, how much you will have at the end of the month, how much in taxes you will pay this year, and how much you will need to retire? If the answer is no to one or all of the above, then buckle up because we have a lot of work to do. But please do not despair. After reading this book you'll be able to brag to your friends and tell them all about compound interest, money markets, and investing smart, but more importantly, you'll be able have full control of your money.

Let's first understand why we need to do this. There are many reasons why it's important to have a great understanding of your finances. First, knowledge is power and understanding your finances will give you the freedom you need to make the right decisions. Second, you can maximize earnings by learning financial concepts, investment vehicles, and tax deductions. Third, it gives you the tools and instruments needed to develop your life passion instead of feeling 'stuck' on an unfulfilling job. Money, as an instrument (not as the end goal), will help you achieve your dreams quicker. Undoubtedly, money and finances scare a lot of people because things that we don't understand frighten us. As a result, we create all kinds of excuses to feel negatively about it. Well, this section, along with your will and efforts, will help you lose the fear by taking control of your expenses.

In this step I provide knowledge that you can find anywhere on the internet. But what I have done is two-fold: I've explained all of these concepts in ways that are easy for a person without previous knowledge on finances to understand; and, I've included them in these 25 steps to plan a gap year because I believe that it will help you get to your destination sooner and stronger. Nonetheless, I strongly recommend that you talk to a financial advisor for any questions that you may have concerning your personal situation.

How often should you be reconciling your finances? In reality, you should be already doing this on a weekly or monthly basis. If you aren't, take this as an opportunity and learn the most you can about managing your personal budget. Possibly an appointment with a bookkeeper may be all the push you need to set you straight and to learn how to manage your money better. Constantly look for ways to maximize your tax deductions. Learn about all the benefits that your current employer provides and that you might be unaware of, such as equity compensation. Additionally, there are many great resources, books, audiobooks, and podcasts written and created by experts that will guide you in the right direction and will provide very valuable teachings on the subject. One of my absolute favorites is a podcast called "Best in Wealth Podcast" by my good friend Scott Wellens. Scott and I worked together at a telecommunications firm back in 2006 and, besides being funny and a standup human being, one of his best qualities was always his ability to teach and mentor others. Because of this, I am not surprised in the least that his podcast has done so well; you can tell he's passionate about educating and helping others. In an attempt to not be biased, I researched a lot of resources that would best explain the practical aspect of creating a budget. Nonetheless, each time I kept coming back to one of Scott's episodes, "Set Up a Budget in 7 Steps", which is episode #137 of his podcast. He explains so clearly the steps that need to be taken, as well as the reasons why it's important for anybody, regardless of their present financial situation, to create a budget. The easiest way to find his content and credentials is by going to www.bestinwealth.com. As follows, just a brief outline of what he recommends doing:

- List out the expenses that you incur in on a monthly basis using categories. Add or remove categories based on your situation, this is just an example to help you out:
  - Car Maintenance
  - Clothing
  - Debt
  - Food
  - Fun, Entertainment
  - Giving (Donations, Charity)
  - Health Insurance
  - Miscellaneous
  - Mortgage/Rent
  - Savings
  - Utilities

- Add up irregular expenses, those which do not happen every month (car insurance, property taxes, water bill, Christmas and birthday gifts) and divide them by 12. Escrow that amount, on a monthly basis.

- Work on a budget adjustment. Add everything up and assess whether you budgeted too much or too little on each category. How do you do that? By comparing what you thought you were going to spend on that category (your budget) and what you actually spent on it (your actual expenses). Recalibrate according.

- Be proactive by tracking your expenses daily using any platform of your choice. You can just do it in Excel or Quicken but Every Dollar makes the process fun. I know, it sounds like an oxymoron, but their app makes the process that easy.

- Assess monthly but check in as often as needed.

- Don't forget to celebrate your financial achievements, even if small. You are now in control!

Once you feel comfortable with the process of tracking your expenses and categorizing them as described above by Scott, proceed with the travel-related aspect of it and mark those items that will not be expenses while you travel (i.e.: utilities). Also, identify those expenses that you can immediately eliminate or considerably reduce (i.e.: clothing) and redirect them to your travel fund. Create a 'Year Off' fund, which will be the newest (and most important) category of your budget makeover. This exercise will help you have a better understanding of what your expenses will be while abroad. More about this on Step 7, Calculate How Much Money You Will Need.

Check all the advice provided on all the episodes on Scott's podcast - they're a great resource in understanding the importance of saving for retirement and the steps that anyone can take to secure financial freedom. The best part is that you can listen to it on the go and share it with whoever you think could use his recommendations.

Also, any financial education tool offered by Fidelity is, in my book, considered top notch. On their website, www.fidelity.com, look for information that provides retirement guidance and a retirement calculator so that you can understand whether you are or not on track with your retirement savings. More importantly, don't be discouraged if you realize that you're not on track. The planning of this sabbatical year might be the best thing that could have happened to you as you now take proactive action to improve your financial life.

You can now feel confident that you have the power to be in control of your money. This is one of the most important steps in the planning of a gap year. If you feel overwhelmed, trust me, it gets easier. Very quickly, you'll be an expert in budgeting but more importantly, you will have a very defined goal to work towards. Having a clear objective is a game-changer.

AUDIO/BOOK RECOMMENDATION: I don't know if you know who Gary Vee is or not. His full name is actually Gary Vaynerchuk and, undoubtedly, none of what I've decided to pursue (way before the inception of this book) could have been accomplished without his teachings. It's one thing to have an idea in your mind that you know is fantastic and you feel very passionate about, but something completely different to have somebody push you (through his books and lessons) to act on them because doing so is guaranteed to bring you happiness. This dude might be as intense as his reputation suggests, but I happen to love his personality and he's the type of push that I needed to believe in myself and to make all of my dreams into reality. Everything he says confirms my perspective in a way that's eerie because sometimes I think he can read my mind, even though we've never met, and he doesn't even know I exist! It's scary yet very comforting all at once. Anything that he writes or says I would recommend. The audio book that turned my life around was Crushing It! You should check it out.

TASK 5.1

Write down in one sentence how you would describe your financial self up to this point. Right underneath, write down the ideal financial you, who you want to work towards becoming.

TASK 5.2

Go through the past 6 months to 1 year of bank statements. Reference the sub-list "Money-Related" that you started back on Step 1 and identify all of the expenses that you can eliminate immediately. Also, work on lowering costs or negotiating a better deal on everything else that cannot be eliminated such as credit card interest rates. Early on you started a rather practical form of minimalism. On this step, commence your financial minimalism. Start your strongest financial foundation to date yet, with no judgements about the past 'you'.

Sub-List
From Step 1

(1) **Money-Related**
a. Cut off
b. Lower costs or negotiate

Section 1 of Table 5

TASK 5.3

From the list of expenses, identify your non-negotiables and ensure that they are part of your main list from Step 1 so you don't lose sight of them. An example of this could be the monthly contribution to your parents' nursing home. Write down everything that you have to account for and set funds aside for two years' worth, if that's a possibility. Know the lifespan of these obligations.

TASK 5.4

Add up all your loans and credit card debts and understand how much you owe. Start paying off by getting a part-time job or a side hustle if necessary. Create a plan: some people prefer paying the smallest debt first and work their way up; some people prefer to pay off those debts with the highest interest rate. The choice is yours but set money aside every month to pay a little bit at a time. This right here is where good money habits are formed. Step 8 will provide additional ideas to increase your current influx of funds.

TASK 5.5

Follow Scott's recommended steps of creating a budget based on categories. Create a "Year Off" category and start saving all you can. Mark those expenses that you will not incur in as you travel and redirect them to your newly created "Year Off" category. This category will be, going forward, your main focus.

Create 1, 5, and 10-Year Plans

Imagine this, you get in your car to drive to a party at a house that you have never been to before. You start driving even though you don't know the address, don't know how to get there, and can't ask friends for directions because none of them knows. How long do you think it will take you to get to the party? You have one guess. That's right, you won't ever get there.

Living life is no different. Most of us go through the motions by breathing and following the crowd, doing what is expected of us based on our age, gender, and geography. There is nothing wrong with that; in fact, it works for most people because it's easier than the alternative. Once in a while you may encounter an inner voice telling you that you're not happy working at this or that job, that life is much more than what you see right now, that you could and should be earning a lot more money than you are making right now. But it's easier to just keep 'driving' in your lane and silently ignore your honest self.

But what if you took charge and decided that from now on you will live your life on your own terms? And that maybe by doing so, by doing what you feel passionate about, you might make more money than you thought possible? Inevitable, we attract abundance when do what we love, as long as we back up this energy with a solid plan. If you could never fail, what, who, and where would you want to be in the next year, five years, ten years? This is a tougher question than you think; it may take some time to answer, but the act of considering it and actively working towards it is what will set you free. As part of this step's exercise, I want you to start thinking about what does 'living on your own terms' mean to you?

Have you ever seen on TV when wild animals are finally set free after being cared for in a confined space for all their lives? Even though the cage is open, even though there is no imminent danger, they will still hesitate or might not even leave their cages at all. That is exactly what happens to our brains the moment we realize all of the freedom we have to do whatever we want to do and become. It is paralyzing in some cases, but we need to aim to understand how to better manage all of this newfound freedom so it's not so overwhelming. Of course, you want to be realistic about how big you want to dream and what you want to become. If you are not great at engineering or math, get seasick or carsick, and want to be an astronaut, that's not likely to happen and you know it. If you have never played basketball professionally, chances to make it to the NBA are not great. On the other hand, if you are not a professional cook but you love cooking and dream of collecting the best recipes of every country that you visit and putting them in a book format, that is absolutely doable. As you start thinking about your 1-year goals, begin making a list of all the reasons why you think you cannot work towards your dream. Any excuse that comes to your head, big or small, write it down. As you go through this book and as you complete the tasks in every chapter, you'll start gaining confidence in yourself as you learn that you can do anything you set your mind to do. Then start scratching off every single one of the excuses you listed and start liberating yourself. This right here is what it means to 'live life on your own terms'.

For the time being, ignore all the internal noise (the self-doubt, guilt of past mistakes, etc.) and the external challenges (money, personal situation, etc.) and work on creating your 1-year plan. Set a goal of who you want to become and write it down in your notebook. Do the same for your 5 and 10-year goals. Be flexible enough to understand that these goals may change as you evolve and it's perfectly okay to change your mind about anything at any point. Remember that party you were trying to get to earlier? Now with these plans in place, getting there should be much easier. Your planning should include at least three aspects: (1) Your journey. Based on the passion that you want to pursue while traveling: Who do you want to be known as in a year or so? (2) Your personal traits. What aspects of yourself you want to improve? and (3) Your financial life. How much debt do you need to pay off? How much do you want to save? How much do you want to make?

Create a 1, 5 and a 10-Year Plan

JOURNEY GOALS	1-YEAR	5-YEARS	10-YEARS
What aspect(s) of yourself do you want to improve on?			
What internal obstacles will you work towards overcoming?			

PERSONAL GOALS	1-YEAR	5-YEARS	10-YEARS
What is the purpose you want to give to your trip?			
What do you want to become an expert on?			

FINANCIAL GOALS	1-YEAR	5-YEARS	10-YEARS
What monetary goals will you work hard to achieve?			
How much money do you want to earn as a digital nomad?			

Table 8:

To bring this full circle, let's go back to the life passion (or more than one, if applicable) that you decided will be the main topic of your travels. Re-phrase each of these passions from a selfish perspective and also from a selfless perspective in this manner:

Selfish passion

Example: I want to learn about the seven wonders of the world, including their history and evolution. I want to be able to see them and appreciate them in person. I want to do this because traveling and learning about the seven wonders of the world brings me joy.

- To every answer you give, ask yourself the 'why', over and over, until you get to the bottom of it. When you do, you'll likely find the answers to a lot of other things. For example, 'why does learning about this bring me joy'? Whatever the answer is to each question, keep asking why.

Selfless passion

Example: I want to show to the world the beauty of the seven wonders and I want to share with everybody this incredible adventure. It would be my dream to inspire others to want to explore the world as well.

- Same here. Ask yourself 'why' several times. For example, "why do I want to inspire others"?

Doing this exercise will help you verbalize the reasons why you love doing something. Moving these reasons from your unconscious brain into your consciousness and then into your heart will allow you to buy into the reasons why you are doing what you are doing. It will make overcoming obstacles and challenges easier because you will have a laser focus on what you're looking to accomplish and why you want to do it. Above all, it will put things into perspective as you now learn to consider your passion as your compass for the rest of your actions. This reminder will come into play every time you second guess yourself and question why you left a steady income for a year of travel. The answer should lie on the fact that you were never truly happy performing whatever job you were doing (or you were dissatisfied with your current life, etc.), and that your search for happiness should be your only mission in life. You owe that to yourself and to everyone around you.

As you are going through this exercise, refer back to your 'power words' - the three adjectives that you selected in Step 2, and ensure that they are aligned with what you are now exploring. In other words, if you have selected "influential", the way that you will explore monetization might be slightly different than if you're driven by the word "revolutionary". Neither is better or worse, they just help you look at your passions and the way to monetize them slightly differently such that it's more in alignment with your true self. In essence, you want to ensure that you are able to identify your drivers and that you don't lose sight of them as you are developing other aspects of your journey.

This exercise will make your 1, 5, and 10-year planning a lot more realistic and achievable.

AUDIO/BOOK RECOMMENDATION: I think that the most inspiring audio book about money and planification that I have listened to has been *6 Months to 6 Figures* by Peter K. Voogd. He's intense, he does not sugar-coat things, and I like that.

Every time I listen to it, it makes me want to get off my chair and take action. He made his first million in his mid 20's and he compiled all his learnings in the book. I hope it inspires you as much as he did me.

TASK 6.1

For each of the passions that you have identified as the main topic of your travels, write down a selfish reason and also a selfless reason why you want to pursue them, as described in a few paragraphs above. This will help you put things into perspective and build your 1, 5, and 10-year planning more attainable.

TASK 6.2

Write down the journey goal, the personal goal, and the financial goal that you will commit to achieving in 1 year, starting now.

TASK 6.3

As you go through this book, think about what your 5 and 10-year plans could look like. Dream as big as you can but be realistic. For instance, I always dreamed of being a ballet dancer but, physiologically, it's not a realistic goal for me. On the other hand, learning and documenting about all the traditional dances in the world and their origins is a 10-year goal that I can stand behind.

Calculate How Much Money You Will Need

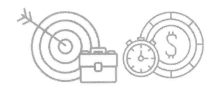

Traveling the world and doing what you love is not free, unfortunately. However, the travel industry spends billions in marketing to make us think that we need to be millionaires to travel the world. In addition to this, we have been conditioned to keep working the 9 to 5 and to stop doing so seems completely outrageous. How will you support yourself without a job? How will you be able to travel without a steady income? I'm here to tell you that it will entail a lot of work on your part, but it is completely possible - many people do it - people who once started where you currently are. I was one of them, and now I'm living the lifestyle I've always wanted. It was not an overnight project and I am not rich, but I do have what I need to travel the world and experience cultures in ways that not many have the luxury to live. I can attest from personal experience that it is so achievable and rewarding that you will ask yourself why you didn't start sooner.

Before we dive deep into money topics, it's important to provide the following disclaimer: even though I still hold a stock trader license (Series 7) and held a CEP certification at some point (Certified Equity Professional), I am not a financial advisor or a CFP (Certified Financial Planner) and I cannot (or will not) provide personal investment advice. You can find the upcoming information anywhere on the internet but I'm just providing it to you in a way that is meaningful to all the efforts that you are making in order to afford a livelihood while you travel the world.

In my 11 years working as a financial specialist, I learned that the relationship we all have with money is dependent upon the purpose we give it and how knowledgeable we are about it, and not how much of it we have -or don't have. If you have a lot of money but don't know how to invest it wisely or don't know much about it, your relationship with it becomes very volatile and toxic. If you don't have much of it, don't know much about money and finances, and believe that having lots of it should be your end goal in life, your relationship with it is probably very unhealthy. You hold the power, but that power is based on your willingness to learn about finances and the purpose you give money. Even if you have debt or even if you think you can't get ahead, learn all you can about money, but above all, learn how to use it as a means to do what you love doing, and not as the end goal. After all, when you're old and ready to kick the bucket, all that you will take with you will be the beautiful memories of your experiences, your travels, the people you met, the people you loved. Everything else that you leave behind such as money or material possessions will mean absolutely nothing.

My intent in covering this section is for you to think of money as an instrument that will help you achieve your dreams rather than a void in your life. Once you understand that, let go of your fears, and take it as a strategic game. You'll be empowered to be creative, generate more of it, and attract it, since you will no longer see money as a threat or something that you are lacking. Little by little, you will start making better financial decisions and acquiring healthier money habits.

I understand that all of our situations are different and that some of us have obligations that we can't get out of and many other reasons why we shouldn't move forward with planning a gap year and travel the world. After all, it does take a huge leap of faith to believe that everything will be alright and that we'll find a way. If you are anything like me, it's difficult for me to not know. I need to have everything planned and figured out because as much as I appreciate that the universe unfolds the way it should, I feel very uneasy leaving the next meal to fate. I used to be more relaxed in that regard when I was younger, but the American dream has trained me to know when to expect things, and it's hard now to live in the moment like I used to. It all comes down to creating life balance, I suppose. Because of this, I calculated how much money I was going to need in order to pay for the things at home while abroad (plus six months, just in case, but more on this in Step 13), and how much money I was going to need while traveling. Additionally, I researched and interviewed a lot of people who travelled extensively to find ways to spend the least amount possible while on the road.

As we saw in Step 5, creating a budget based on spending categories will allow you to have control of your money and thus increase your assets and lower your liabilities. This, in turn, will allow you to save as much as possible. Stop all the unnecessary spending and make a solid plan to pay off debts. Calculating how much money you will need to set aside to pay for things at home while abroad is a very personal exercise. Once you figure that out, add six months to it. This is your emergency fund. You will have those funds available upon your return. This will allow you to get back on your feet should you decide to come back to home base.

When I was planning my first gap year, I knew I couldn't afford much in terms of hotels and meals, at least at the beginning. Therefore, I researched organizations around the world that could connect me with hosts from different countries who offer free room and board in exchange for volunteer hours. These are legit organizations and I provide all the details about them in Step 16. The main lesson here is to know that room and board does not have to be an expense for which you need to save a huge amount of money if you are willing to volunteer 20 to 25 hours a week in the area that you want to travel. Even if you want to go this route, I'd still recommend saving money for this category just in case things fall through, because nothing is guaranteed in this world. But also know that it is not impossible to travel the world with just a few dollars in your pocket.

Here is a list of the items that you might want to consider saving for and which you will need to account for while traveling. It's a very rough estimate, depending on where you are going. Asia is the most economical region (except for Japan, which I'd put at par with Europe), followed by Latin

America, Africa, and the Middle East. Europe is most certainly the priciest, followed by North America. Feel free to add to it as you plan your own journey. Not only the region or regions that you're planning on going but also the number of countries that you're visiting will have an impact on the amount of money that you will need to save. I cannot give you an estimate of what that will be because it will all depend on your journey. Based on what you will be doing, you may want to stay in one country the entire time. Or, like myself, maybe you want to stay in a country per month. Here is a rough estimate of what I thought I would need on my own very first gap year to Latin America:

- Country exit fees: $300
- Initial and final airfare: $2,000
- Room meals not covered by volunteer work: $5,000
- Tours and adventures: $1,500
- Transportation between countries: $2,500 (bus, plane, train)
- Transportation within each country: $1,500 (bus, taxi, train)
- Travel medical insurance: $1,000
- Vaccines: $1,000
- Visas: $200

Total (1 year): $15,000 (+ $5,000 emergency)

It helps tremendously to have a rough idea, even if just within the ballpark, of how little is needed to get by for a year of international travel if you don't mind volunteer work and being frugal so that you can pursue your dreams. It could potentially be much cheaper than living at home. It is for me, as crazy as it sounds. Having an emergency fund is also very important as it will give you the confidence of knowing that you'll be covered should something come up. Whatever your total is, which should include your 'emergency while abroad' fund, this should be your goal amount under the "Year Off" category that you created on your budget planning exercise from Step 5.

AUDIO/BOOK RECOMMENDATION: If things are starting to get a little bit overwhelming, a really good source of inspiration that I find myself listening to over and over is *The Daily Edge* by David Horsager. It's not necessarily related to money, but rather about increasing efficiency. It helps me declutter my brain, thus allowing me to make better financial decisions. The full title of the book is The Daily Edge: Simple Strategies to Increase Efficiency and Make an Impact Every Day. I think that says it all.

TASK 7.1

At this point, it might be a little too early just yet to determine how much you will need while abroad, but you should have a pretty good idea about the kind of money that you will need to maintain things at your home base while traveling. If you don't, start adding things up and keep updating your main list as things come up. Save and earn more during your planning stage by reading and following the recommendations of the next step, Step Up Your Money Game.

STEP 8

Step Up Your Money Game

At this point, you should be working to have your finances under control. In Step 5 we discussed the importance of creating a budget and saving the most you can. Based on Step 7, you now have a very general idea about how much money you will need in order to travel for an entire year, give or take, depending on the region you want to go to. Back in the section "What Is a Digital Nomad and How Do You Become One?" we briefly discussed the three options to get you going financially into the world of travel and freedom. The options are (A) Save enough money before you leave, (B) Work virtually while you travel; and (C) Create your digital shop. The goal of this section is to provide a deeper dive into each of these paths. Not one is better than the other. They're just different and you'll have to decide which one is best for you. You could pursue all three if you feel ambitious, but most people just opt for one or two.

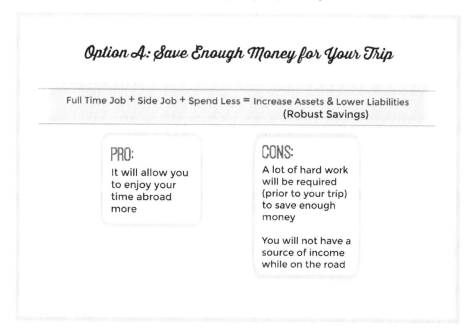

Table 9

Option A: <u>Save Enough Money for Your Trip</u>. Undoubtedly, we all should be working towards a healthy financial situation. In an ideal world, this means having no debt and building a savings fund. Realistically speaking, sometimes it's not that easy. But the truth is, we all could be doing a lot more than what we're doing right now to step up our money game. As you hold a full-time job, you could have a side gig that can generate additional income. I hate to be the one to say it, but if you use all those hours spent in front of the television or on social media driving for Uber, Uber Eats, or Lyft instead, you could easily increase your monthly income by at least $1,000 dollars. Easily. As we saw in Step 7, that is roughly the bare minimum that you would need to travel cheaply for a year, as long as you're willing to do part-time volunteer work, thus getting free room and board (details on Step 9).

But likely, up until this point there wasn't a real incentive for you to work extra hard and get a side gig. Now that you've discovered what your life passion is and are ready to conquer the world, I'm sure that you'll be much more efficient with your time and you won't mind sacrificing leisure time for the sake of seeing the world. As follows, there are a few suggestions that you can start putting into practice immediately to increase your assets column:

- Buy fixer uppers. Fix them up, re-sell them or rent them out, and repeat.
- Call all your creditors and service vendors and negotiate a better interest rate.
- Drive for Lyft, Uber, Uber Eats, or DoorDash.
- Find a higher paying job or work with your employer towards a salary increase.
- Get a second part time job.
- Invent something and patent it.
- Own real estate that you can rent out.
- Park any cash that you may have in a high yielding money market.
- Start selling things (new or used) on Etsy, Amazon, eBay.
- Transcribe, or caption videos at Rev.com. Extra pay if you know a foreign language.
- Voice over acting.
- When your car lease is over, consider paying cash for an older (yet reliable) car so that you don't have a monthly car payment.

When I was laid off in 2018, I had a choice to make. I knew I needed to straighten my finances, but I also wanted to create my own brand. Building a business was going to take time;

therefore, I knew I had to look for regular employment for at least a year in order to pay off my debts and save money. I then accepted a job that paid well but never stopped working towards my own business. Sometimes it was challenging because the stress of my full-time job was so high (mostly because I was very unhappy in it) that when I'd get home from work I was both mentally and physically drained. Yet knowing that in less than two years I could be traveling the world was enough motivation for me to work long hours on my business, including weekends and holidays. By August of 2019 I had paid off my debts and saved enough money to be able to sustain myself for at least 6 months into traveling. This included family financial obligations such as my mom's nursing home.

At this point, I felt that I was in an okay place if I wanted to travel, but it was not yet optimal. This meant that I needed to find other ways to support my travels (spoiler alert, I went with Option C). However, if you are able to pull it off with the savings you currently have, then power to you. Then when you are able to take that year off, all you have to do is focus on your passion, the topic of your travels, and enjoy life. For the rest of us, there is more work to do.

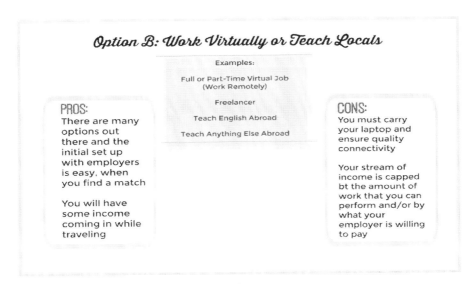

Table 10

Option B: <u>Work Virtually or Teach Locals</u>. According to a statistic from www.flexjobs.com, as of February of 2020, roughly 4.7 million people work remotely. That's an increase of over 200% compared to what was documented in 2005. This percentage became much higher when Covid 19 hit globally. Pandemic and safety aside however, the trend is gradually increasing because it makes sense from an employee satisfaction perspective and from an employer overhead savings viewpoint. This is, of course, a generalization because depending on the nature of the business or a manager's measurement of productivity and expectations, it's not realistic for all industries to acquire this business model. But know that there are many companies out there that are looking for employees who are willing to work remotely and that search will continue to increase many-fold.

Freelancing is similar but not the same. When you have a particular skill or certification - for instance, you're a programmer, graphic designer, translator, writer, editor, or anything along those lines - you can subscribe to platforms that can connect you with people looking to hire you for work. There's much more flexibility in being a freelancer than being employed as a remote worker, but at the same time, the influx of work could potentially be irregular at best.

Lastly, English teachers are always in demand. If you'd rather be in one place for the duration for your gap year, then you may want to consider this line of work. The main upside of this as a strategy is that you have the tremendous opportunity to learn the local language… for free. There are many organizations out there that connect schools in various countries with individuals willing to teach. Make sure that you check requirements as soon as you can since many of them might require the TEFL certification (Teaching English as a Foreign Language) which you can obtain during your planning stage. Be mindful, however, that this certificate usually runs for about $1,000 dollars and you'll need 150 hours of online coursework. Prestigious organizations such as CIEE.org can guide you best and point you in the right direction.

Here's a list that I snatched from a social media group that I belong to. I'm not affiliated with any of the below sites and I don't receive a commission on any of them. As of the publishing of this book all links worked properly and were legitimate, to the best of my knowledge and research.

Work Remotely:
www.weworkremotely.com/
www.flexjobs.com/
www.remote.co/remote-jobs/
www.remotive.io/
www.skipthedrive.com/
www.workingnomads.co/jobs
www.virtualvocations.com
www.remoteok.io/

www.jobspresso.co/
www.workingnomads.co/jobs
www.jobscribe.com/
www.outsourcely.com/remote-workers
www.landing.jobs/
www.authenticjobs.com/
www.dribbble.com/jobs
www.angel.co/
www.stackoverflow.com/jobs/get-started
www.jobs.github.com/positions?description=&location=Remote
Freelance Sites:
www.toptal.com/
www.fiverr.com/
www.upwork.com/
www.guru.com/
www.freelancer.com/
www.freelancermap.com/
www.coworks.com/
Teach English Abroad:
www.ciee.org/go-abroad/work/teach-english-
abroadwww.jetprogramme.org/
www.teachaway.com/uae-government-schools
www.teachaway.com/teach-english-korea/epik-english-program-korea-
public-school-jobs-korea
www.teachaway.com/explore-program
Teach English Online:
www.teachaway.com/
www.vipkid.com/
www.teachaway.com/schools/dada
www. teacher.qkids.net/
www. itutorgroup.com/
www.teacher.gogokid.com/
www.51talk.com
www.englishuntusa.com/

There are many advantages to becoming a remote
employee or freelancer, or even teaching English online. You
can literally be anywhere in the world, create your own
schedule and work on your own terms, as long as you have a
laptop and reliable internet connection. The pay may or may
not be great, but you'll at least have some sort of income
coming in. Room and board in places like Asia are so

economical that you can live comfortably with very little for a while. Of course, like everything, there are downfalls too. The amount of money that you can potentially make is capped by what your employer pays you. If you're a freelancer, you might be limited to the amount of work that you are willing and able to accept. Depending on what your goals are, this may leave little time to explore your passions, the reason why you've decided to travel the world, your driver to take the time off. At the end of the day, you have to create some sort of balance between the time you're willing to give to someone and the time you allot to yourself to pursue your own dreams. Don't forget that your top priority should be the life passion that you're chasing - that is the main reason you're doing what you're doing.

Option C: Create a Digital Shop

(Your Passion + World Travel = Endless Content) + Your Offering = Source of Income

PROS:	CONS:
If built correctly, there is no cap to the earnings and stream of income that your shop could generate	Setting up your digital shop is a lot of work
You will be building your own personal brand	Depending on the offering(s) that you create, as well as the upkeep, you might have to work hard (at least initially) while traveling
Your time abroad will be mostly spent on your passion, as it becomes the topic of your trip	

Table 11

Option C: Create a Digital Shop. This option is undoubtedly very challenging yet the most rewarding one of all. Creating a digital shop means to create an offering that has the potential to generate money and that it's closely related to your passion. This is designed, developed, and put into practice during the planning stage, and, if profitable, this could generate a great source of income while you travel. Examples of these offerings are online courses, coaching or consulting services, e-books, affiliate marketing, a YouTube channel, paid speeches, etc. Anything that does not require a physical product and can be somewhat automated can be qualified as a digital offering. Many, erroneously, refer to this as passive income. It's far from it. Depending on the offering that you embark on, there might be some 'passive' aspects to the way that the funds come in; however, some sort of maintenance in the way of digital marketing or otherwise needs to exist for the offering to sell regularly. Should you choose this path, you may want to set things up as early in your planning stage as possible, because it takes a while for things to get going. You will have to work a lot to get this up and running, but the way you'll feel once you do and start reaping the fruit of what you sowed is just incredible. One of the most rewarding aspects of this process is the ability to reach your target audience and help them solve a problem that they may have or inspire them to do something.

Once you decide on the offering, you want to set up a platform where you can display it. Think of it as having baked the most amazing chocolate cake you've ever made but you need a venue to display it in so that people can look at it, admire it, and hopefully buy a piece of it if that's what they're looking for. That venue could be your website, Facebook, TikTok, Instagram, Pinterest page, etc.

Next, you need 'fliers and balloons' to attract visitors to your venue, right? Otherwise, how would they know what you have to offer? Those 'fliers and balloons' are the content that you create around your offering which are related to the passion you're looking to develop abroad - the topic of your travels. This is why traveling the world gives you an infinite canvas not just to explore and develop your passion, but to produce the content that will attract people to your offering. Here's where you help people understand how you can solve a challenge that they may have, or how you can improve their lives, or how you can entertain them, etc. In essence, through your fliers and balloons, you're letting the world know who your target audience is and what your niche is.

Lastly, you will need a form of digital marketing and advertisement so that each and every person who likes 'chocolate cake', can receive an invitation to look at, taste a sample of, and hopefully buy a piece of your delicious creation.

Let me give you an example of an outstanding digital shop. There's a digital marketing course geared towards individuals and business owners to learn social media marketing and branding online. Nate and Hannah Buchan own this business and they call themselves The Creatives Platform (www.thecreativesplatform.com). They are both from New Zealand and have been traveling the world for several years. What they've done is brilliant. They've created a digital course (several, actually) which anybody can enroll in and take at their own pace and in the convenience of their own home. For my own research, I enrolled in one of their courses (Get Branded Mastery Course) and I have to say that I was very impressed. Each lesson is accompanied by a video and they take turns explaining the subject matter with clear examples and personal stories. I learned a lot, I must say. All of this is prerecorded and built in a platform that allows people from all over the world to access from anywhere, after payment has been processed. In the meantime, Nate and Hanna pursue their respective passions (Hannah is a blogger at Intrepid Introvert, and Nate is a consultant at World Nate) yet they're very active on promoting their courses all year round via digital marketing; however, they also create a great deal of free content through their respective blogs.

Their work is fantastic, and you should definitely check their courses out, especially if you need to learn about digital marketing. But my point in showcasing them as an example of what a digital shop is because they:

- Follow their respective passions (Hannah: travel for introverts; Nate: world adventures and digital marketing consultation)
- Create content related to their passions. This content attracts traffic to their offering (Hannah & Nate: through their blogs)
- Define their target audiences through their content (Hannah: introverts; Nate: individuals and business owners)
- Have an offering that generates income (Hannah & Nate: The Creatives Platform courses)
- Display their offering in a teaching platform (Teachable) but also on their respective websites, which directs people to their teaching platform.
- Use social media to direct traffic to their offering through digital marketing (Facebook Ads) based on the targeted audience.

This business model works very well for Hannah and Nate, and it's proven to be extremely successful, not only from a financial perspective, but also from a freedom and passion exploration perspective. More importantly, they've helped thousands of individuals solve their problem (understanding digital marketing) and just as many businesses (helping them strategize marketing to make more money). Not only that, but they have also built The Creatives Platform Community Facebook private group for those who have purchased any of their online courses. Now, could it get better than this for a digital nomad? I think not.

In the next section "Elements of a Digital Shop" we'll look at the main concepts and aspects that you need to know regarding opening a digital shop, which will help you generate income while on the road. For now, I mostly wanted to provide the three alternatives to funding a year off without requiring you to be a millionaire. In fact, every day, regular people like you and I find ways to start traveling the world with very limited funds. Some of them (including myself) spend an excruciating amount of time and effort on the front end to build something that eventually has the potential to generate a pretty nice source of income. Will you be next?

AUDIO/BOOK RECOMMENDATION: This is one of my favorite audio books and probably the one I have listened to more times than the others. It's called Being Boss by Kathleen Shannon and Emily Thompson. This book is about owning who you are, knowing what you want, and making it happen, which is in essence what you are doing right now. I hope you enjoy it as much as I do.

TASK 8.1

Start contemplating which of the three options is most suitable for you: saving enough funds, working remotely/freelancing, or creating your own digital shop. Regardless, you should start stepping up your money game by avoiding unnecessary spending and by saving the most you can. If you're thinking about opening a digital shop, start thinking about what type of offering you could develop, what problem can you solve, how can you help your target audience. Remember to relate your offering to the life passion that you have or are in the process of exploring.

ELEMENTS OF A DIGITAL SHOP

In order of appearance, all of the concepts mentioned below are important in their own way. These are the highlights and the bare minimum of what you need to know to build your own digital shop. I am no expert on it but having recently gone through all of this as a novice has allowed me to identify those elements that were new to my vocabulary and needed to learn about. My viewpoint is fresh since I had no prior experience until I started creating my own digital shop. There is certainly a lot to learn about digital marketing, however, the following is a good starting point. The truth is that the beginning was overwhelming for me because the internet is overloaded with information, and few places give you the basics. That's the purpose of this section: to help you avoid the hurdles I went through when figuring out what I needed to figure out. There are tons of books about each of the below topics, all written by experts. I would definitely recommend reading and learning from them. This is just enough to get you in the right direction without overwhelming you unnecessarily.

Probably the best way to explain each of these concepts is by providing a concrete example. For that purpose, I'm going to use the business model of someone who I admire and have learned a lot from this past year, Cathrin Manning. The name of her website is The Content Bug (www.thecontentbug.com). Even though she's not a digital nomad (I'm sure she could be if she wanted to) I chose her because she clearly hit on all the elements I wanted to cover here and she's one of the most multifaceted digital entrepreneurs I've seen. The fact that her own focus is digital marketing had no bearing on my choice. Nevertheless, I think that her content is on point! It's worth noting that I do not receive an affiliate commission from her. Let's dive in.

Passion. As we learned in Step 2, Identify Your Passion, it's necessary to identify what inspires you - what makes you happy. The main reason for this is because our goal in life should be to be happy and, hence, to do things that make us happy. Another reason is because we want to use that focus as the main topic for our travels. My passions are cultural differences and dancing and that's what I focus on when I travel. Cathrin's passions are helping people grow a YouTube channel and help them become digital entrepreneurs. Somebody else's passion could be historical buildings or finding the best dessert recipes from all over the world. What are your passions?

Niche Market & Niche Audience. A niche market is the service you specialize in. This service is provided to a defined subset of a general audience. After identifying your passion (which almost by default becomes your niche market), understand what sector of the universe your topic applies to. Since the ultimate goal is to attract people to your offering, we need to limit the expenditure of resources just to those who our offering applies to. Additionally, focusing on your niche audience (target market) and understanding who they are helps you serve them better. Some of the categories used in understanding a niche market are: demographics (gender, age), psychographics (values, interests, attitudes), and geographics (residents of a certain country, city, or neighborhood). Cathrin's niche market are usually millennials who want to become digital entrepreneurs. However, I'm no millennial and I consume her content just as much. Her niche market and audience are in alignment with her passion - her focus.

Website. Nowadays you must have a website if you want to be taken seriously. All of your credibility is packed in a few pages of digital display for the world to see. The good news is that creating one is very easy nowadays. I was hyper challenged in that regard. In fact, I sat on a WordPress website for almost a year. I finally gave up and switched to GoDaddy and I got it done in a couple of hours and it looks beautiful. There are many other companies that are easy to use as well, such as SquareSpace or Wix. Websites like WordPress are more geared towards people who understand coding and possess the skills required to make a website incredible (or can pay someone to do it). Either way, make sure that your website is easy to navigate, clean, simple and clear. Start defining yourself as a brand. Here's where your content (maybe a blog, maybe just pictures) and your offering will reside. Take a look at Cathrin's website

www.thecontentbug.com for some inspiration.

SEO. SEO stands for Search Engine Optimization. Imagine you're searching for the best beaches in Bali but instead, get results telling you all about all the local plumbers in your area. I don't know about you, but I'd be pretty annoyed. In the grand scheme of things, the main purpose of the SEO is to improve the user experience by filtering out illegitimate websites or websites not related to the search topic, thus increasing the quality of the results for those individuals looking for whatever information that they are searching for. This applies to you because you want to ensure that people (target audience) looking for what you have to offer (niche market) are actually able to be connected to your website. Also, you want your pages to be "optimized" because people would click away if the pictures on your website are too heavy and don't download quickly. We live in times of instant gratification and you need to ensure that your pages download quickly. There are many things that you can actively do to improve your website's SEO score. First, test its health by looking at its SEO through this website www.seoptimer.com. This is a free service and you don't need the pro version for the purpose outlined here. It also provides a list of the things that you could do to increase your website's efficiency. Once your SEO is optimal, let's make friends and bring as many people to it as we possibly can. Cathrin's website's SEO score is an "A" according to the SEO optimizer tool. No surprise there.

Content Creation. Content creation serves many purposes. First and foremost, it should be a way for you to serve your target audience and provide a solution to their needs - filling a gap. Cathrin's content, especially on YouTube

(@CathrinManning), is all about answering questions on how to become a successful YouTuber or a successful digital marketer. The blog on her website is also the reflection of her passion (digital marketing and entrepreneurship). But also, content for some could be a way of expression. For instance, writing about how you feel or what you saw when you visited this or that country, or posting photographs with a caption, might just be all the content that you want to create. Just ensure that it's closely linked to what inspires you.

Offering. There are many options out there, depending on what your cup of tea is. Don't worry, when I first started, I felt like none of them suited me. In fact, I didn't want to have an offering because I felt uncomfortable monetizing on my passion. But I quickly understood that people are looking to pay others for what they value. For instance, you're hungry, running errands and on the road, and need a quick snack. Wouldn't you go to a drive through and pay a couple of dollars for a quick snack? Monetizing on your passion is no different. You have something that others value and want to pay you money for it because your offering will improve their lives in one way or another.

In Cathrin's example, her website contains a section "Shop TCB", where she displays all the digital courses that she has. These courses are excellent, the prices are very reasonable, and her products solve a very specific need for her target audience. What other offerings could you possibly explore and create? There are a few, but before you dismiss them (I know I did when I was first exploring options), know that you don't have to be an expert or a pro... that comes with time. All you have to have is the willingness to learn, fail, practice, try again, and succeed.

Anybody, and I mean anybody, can do any of these. It took me a little bit of time to recognize all of the skills that I had accumulated through my years. My doubts and insecurities sure did a great job of hiding all the good qualities I had in me.

Out of desperation to break out of my cocoon, I started experimenting with a few offerings, including creating YouTube videos, and creating online courses. I am so happy I did because beyond the monetary fruits of my hard labor, I started to feel so much more confident in myself. The shy, socially awkward, and socially anxious me was now comfortable speaking in front of others, posting on social media, and conveying my message to anybody who would listen. I now even give speeches at my local Toastmasters! My point is, don't knock it until you try it. Even if you don't succeed at first, try again and again until you do. Here are a few ideas:

Blogging: regardless whether you monetize on this or not, blogging is a fantastic way to get content out there, which you can post on your website or social media of your choice. Should you choose to monetize on it, here are several ideas. Keep in mind that a few require a physical product, so make sure you choose those options that you can manage while you travel.

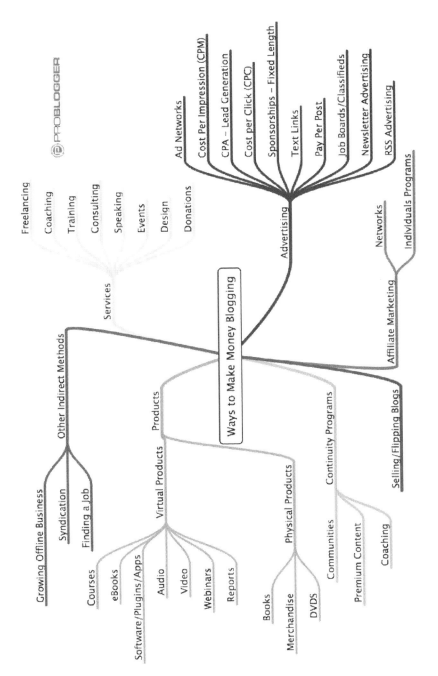

Table 12: *Source: https://problogger.com/how-to-make-money-blogging/*

- Consulting or Coaching Packages: If you have years of experience in a given field, preferably in a field that you are passionate about, have some sort of certificate or degree to prove it, and there's enough demand for it; you could set yourself up to become a consultant. Research what's needed in the form of a marketing package based on your niche and enroll in a scheduling platform such as Calendly, Setmore, or Genbook. Get yourself a reliable video conference platform such as Zoom, Skype (or Skype for Business), GoToMeeting, etc. A robust internet connection will be key when speaking with clients while on the road.
- Cookbooks: I didn't know this, but apparently cookbooks are among the best-selling books of all time. If you have a collection of your favorite recipes based on a special restriction, or ingredient, or locality, then put them together and publish them. For a cookbook part 2, can you imagine collecting recipes from each country that you go to?
- Digital Courses: just like in a classroom, except that you teach online. You can record audio or video in advance and post them on your preferred platform such as Teachable, Udemy, Kajabi.
- Photography: since millions publish content daily, there is a high demand for unique photography. There are photo sites that buy images from creators like you, and you don't have to be a professional photographer either. Fotalia, iStockphoto, Shutterstock, 123RF are some of these companies.
- Patreon: this is a membership-based business where individuals pay you a monthly fee just for you posting anything you want: a podcast, videos, visual arts, written work, tutorials, anything.
- Podcasts: most podcasts are free but some are subscription-based. There are so many platforms out there; some of the best ones are Podbean, BuzzSprout, and Blubrry.

- Tutorials and Guides: Most information can be found for free on the internet. Google and YouTube are the top two search engines. However, there's always going to be a market for organized, in-depth, high quality tutorials and guides. Put something great together and add a merchant account feature to your website so that you can start accepting credit card and PayPal payments.
- YouTube Channel: I added this as a social media, but if done right, YouTube can be a great source of income as well. In fact, check out all Cathrin's YouTube videos about how much she's able to monetize on them. You'll want to start right away! Anybody can create and upload videos but the minimum requirement to be able to monetize on them is that you have to have at least 1,000 subscribers and 4,000 viewing hours. Getting monetized just means that when your video is played by someone and you can get paid by the ads that run in between. If the viewer skips the ad, you don't get paid, but if they watch all the way through, then you do get paid. You get paid even more if the viewer, who was watching your video, clicks on that paid advertisement. I'd say get a few videos up and running before you leave, and work on a regular video content schedule while traveling.

Social Media. Here's where you can connect with people to learn from, help out, or teach. The content that you post on your website could be posted here as well. All of the content you create lets the world know who you are and what you offer, what problem you solve, how funny you can be, how beautiful your pictures are, etc. The goal is to grow a fan base, as this is what will support your brand. You grow a fan base by posting quality content, replying to comments in a professional manner, ignoring hateful comments, 'liking' and commenting on other people's posts that bring value to you, and in general, interacting as much as possible. Building a fan base is important because they will be the first ones to see and try your offering. Likely, they're your target audience. Here they are, in alphabetical order:

Facebook: You could keep your personal Facebook page and post content that way. You could also create a business page which is linked to your personal page. There is no additional cost and followers from your business page will not see your personal page unless you want them to. Facebook has 2.5 billion monthly active users and 1.6 billion mobile daily active users (source: www.omnicoreagency.com).

Instagram: Geared mostly for videos and picture stories, you could post content using your personal Instagram account. Or, you could have your Business Instagram account linked to your business Facebook account and post both at the same time. When I post, I normally open Instagram, choose the pictures, write the caption, make sure I have my hashtags, and select the Facebook radio button so that it posts in both places at the same time. Instagram has 1 billion monthly active users and 500 million daily active users (source: www.omnicoreagency.com)

LinkedIn: Always keep your LinkedIn profile up to date. There is no need to upgrade to Premium unless you really want to. You can upload content just like you do on other social media platforms. There are 310 million monthly active users (source: www.omnicoreagency.com)

Pinterest: There is a certain demographic that still uses Pinterest religiously. Assess whether it makes sense for you to spend time on it or not. There are 335 million monthly active users and 2 million users save pins daily (source: www.omnicoreagency.com)

Snapchat: If you're looking to target a younger crowd, undoubtedly go with TikTok. However, Snapchat's stats are impressive: 360 million monthly active users and 218 million daily active users (source: www.omnicoreagency.com)

TikTok: There is a huge potential with this platform due to all the formats, filters, hashtags, and connections that you create. If you are big on Snapchat and it works for you, great, keep doing what you're doing, but I would strongly recommend that you start getting into TikTok and get comfortable with it. It's here to stay and users' age demographics are increasing slowly but surely. There are 1 billion active users and users use the app 52 minutes daily as an average (source: www.wallaroomedia.com)

Twitter: This is certainly not as used as other platforms, but I'm not wasting free digital real estate if it comes free and easy. All I do is just copy my captions and hashtags, upload my pictures, paste the captions and hashtags, and post. I could turn on the radio button to post to Twitter at the same time that I'm on Instagram, but I noticed that the post does not look great at all. There is still a lot of work to be done in that area, and unless this is a platform that makes sense for your content, I'd skip it altogether. There are 330 million monthly active users and 152 million daily active users (source: www.omnicoreagency.com)

YouTube: This is the second largest search engine, right behind Google. I added YouTube here because it's a social media platform which can efficiently convey your message and your content. I also added it as an offering because enough viewership and subscribers can generate a very nice source of income for you as well. There are 2 billion monthly active users and 5 billion videos watched daily in the world (source: www.omnicoreagency.com)

Since we're talking about social media, let's also talk about hashtags. Don't underestimate their power. Most people know what they are but if you don't, hashtags are those pound symbols that you see on social media posts (#). Hashtags play a crucial role in developing interest in your social media accounts and it helps categorize content for your audience. In other words, hashtags allow people find content that is relevant to their interest. Use them wisely.

Traffic. You've built a website, have posted content there and on social media, and have created your offering. Now what? You need traffic so that people can take a look at what you've created and buy into your offering, if that's what they're looking for. There are two types of traffic: organic and directed. Organic traffic is the traffic that naturally arrives to your page because someone was looking for your content to begin with. Directed traffic is the traffic that results from you applying a certain strategy, which you normally have to pay. Why is this important to know? Because organic traffic is almost nonexistent when you are first starting out, since nobody knows who you are or what your business does. Therefore, you have to create a strategy to (initially) attract traffic to the specific population that you want to target. Cathrin and most influencers use what's called a "lead magnet" on YouTube and on all of her social media real estate. This is simply a teaser, a freebie, such as 10 steps to do this or that, which leads consumers of her free content to her website. Here's where her offering is displayed for anybody to purchase. There are other ways to direct traffic to your website, most often through paid ads.

Promote. You can tell your friends about your website and offering, you can post it on your Facebook page, and you could even create its own Facebook page, but that alone won't produce the level of traffic that you need. You have three options and I recommend doing them all: (1) reference your website across all of your social media handles, (2) advertise using tools such as Facebook Boost or Google AdSense; and/or, (3) create a YouTube channel and promote your product there. This is the most direct way to draw traffic to your website since you're already addressing the audience that's interested in what you do. Please note that before using Facebook Ads or Facebook Boost, you want to learn terms such as remarketing, A/B split testing, audience analysis, and lookalike audiences. Even though Facebook Ads are incredibly cheap for the reach they have, narrowing down your audience will save you a lot of money. The terms listed above will help you do just that.

Remember the importance of knowing your target audience's demographics? Tools from Facebook and Google Ads will allow you to specify all of that so that your advertising dollars are as efficient as they can possibly be. Tracking helps you identify which platform paying customers are most likely to come from. My favorite guy is Kevin David, because he explains it in a way that a beginner can understand. His YouTube channel is @Kevin David. The truth is, at the beginning I had to watch his videos several times, over and over, in order to understand a smidge. But little by little, I started to understand more and now, even though I'm no expert, I can create and run my own ads campaigns.

Tracking. You can track the traffic being directed to your website. Even your website should be able to provide these statistics. In fact, Google has the most robust tracking program, called Google Analytics. Facebook's tracking program is called Pixels. Pixels are pieces of coding (don't worry, you don't need to know how to create them, you just have to know how to copy and paste) that tracks the source of your traffic.

You want to add pixels to your website to be able to analyze where traffic is coming from. Why is that important? Because if the majority of your traffic comes from Facebook, then you want to put a lot more emphasis on creating ads or boosting posts via that site. Google Analytics ID is easy to set up and you'll be able to track the traffic that comes to your website as well. Don't worry, only the source of traffic is tracked, and no personal information is viewable. For instance, the ad that you posted on Facebook directing people to your website is doing great and generating a lot of traffic to your website, which is converting into customers, then you want to continue posting similar ads on Facebook. But if the ad you posted on Instagram is not generating a lot of traffic, or it is generating traffic but it's not converting well (not many people are buying your offering), then you may want to test other posts or simply stop advertising on Instagram. This saves you a lot of money in the long run. To create your Google Analytics ID, you will need your website's URL, that's it.

So, this is digital marketing for zero beginners in a nutshell. I hope this helps you get started with your digital shop. There's so much information out there that there's no excuse to not be able to find the answer to something. The challenge that we're all faced with when we are new at something is that we don't know what we don't know. It's difficult to get started if we don't know the basic concepts. The goal of this section is to provide a high-level introduction so that you can become a successful digital nomad. I can't wait to see what's on your digital shop!

STEP 9

Determine Type of Travel and Accommodations

Type of Travel

By now, you should have a good idea of the reasons you want to see the world and are working hard to get your personal finances in the healthiest shape possible. Additionally, based on the way that you've decided to monetize while on the road, this step will help you determine the type of travel that you will be able to do, at least at the beginning. When you feel more comfortable capitalizing on your content and revenue starts flowing more consistently, you'll be able to have the flexibility and the freedom to stay in any accommodation of your choice as your budget improves.

To understand this correlation better, I've grouped various objectives into four different categories based on what you want to get out of your year off. These categories are: Arts and Crafts; Research and Learning; Volunteer and Service; and, Health and Wellness. I have seen lots of travel books and was most inspired by the idea of grouping objectives into categories. Of course, your interests could fall into more than one category, but the fewer the categories, the more efficient your trip will be. It doesn't mean that you couldn't handle more than one category at a time, it just means that it will be easier to focus on just one thing at a time.

For me, my top goal was 'Research & Learning' because I wanted to document and share specific cultural differences as well as the traditional dances of the countries I visited. I've always been motivated by learning as much as I can, and I recently found my love for sharing my discoveries with the world. At the same time, I was on a tight budget when I started, so I had no choice other than to sign up to volunteer through organizations such as Work Away and World Packers in order to save on room and board (more detail about this in Step 16). Therefore, the purpose of my trip also fell under the category of 'Volunteer & Service'. I didn't mind that at all because I always loved helping others and felt that it would be the perfect way to meet more people from all over the world. Knowing the reasons that I wanted to see the world, the trip categories, and, consequently, the type of accommodations that I needed to seek, gave me much better clarity on the path that I needed to follow.

The goal of conceptualizing your trip in this manner is to allow you to better understand your journey along with the type of accommodations and packing that are more suitable to meet your objectives. Here is a brief description of each of the four categories with corresponding examples, followed by types of accommodations and packing suitable for each.

ARTS & CRAFTS

Due to the historical and geographical differences of each region, arts and crafts from a cultural perspective is such a diverse topic amongst countries. Maybe you want to learn, observe, or even teach the crafts of a specific trade. Or maybe you want to appreciate the fine arts or want to present a specific form of art from one or many cultures from a particular perspective. Here is also where your creativity gets to explore the world in unimaginable ways. The possibilities are endless, but make sure that they are in alignment with your passion.

Examples of activities under this category that you can use to create content:

- Learn a craft particular to a culture
- Teach a craft or artistic skill
- Perform a craft or artistic skill
- Deepen your knowledge about an artist
- Deepen your knowledge about an artistic style or era
- Observe and appreciate an artistic aspect of a culture
- Attend writing workshops
- Go to carnivals and festivals typical of the region
- Visit a specific type of museum or art-related institutions within a continent
- Use the various cultures or geographies as the canvas for your photography, film, drawing, painting, etc.

RESEARCH & LEARNING

For some, brain stimulation through exploration and learning is a vital aspect of their lives. Some would argue that there is no happiness in their lives if some form of mind expansion is not present. Luckily, if you fall into this category, only the sky is the limit especially when you're traveling the world. There are even learning retreats that you can partake in, should you feel the need to enrich your current area of expertise or take on a new skill. Some of these trips are organized and led by professors or top experts in their fields of study. Or maybe, you need to explore the world on your own to understand in which line of work you feel more fulfilled.

Examples of activities under this category that you can use to create content:

- Learn to cook the cuisine of a specific region
- Teach how to make your world-famous [fill in the blanks]
- Research the different religions and customs of a region
- Learn about a specific aspect of an area such as animal or plant species

VOLUNTEER & SERVICE

There are volunteer activities that will help your heart find the way to a life of selflessness and fulfillment. Maybe you've reached a point in your life where you need to find meaning or need to re-discover yourself. Maybe you desperately need to reassess life and you know that helping others will bring things into perspective. Whatever the reasons are, there are many resources that you can tap into that will help you achieve your goals. Beware of organizations such as Adventures Within

Reach or Free-a-Child where you have to pay a hefty amount in order to be a volunteer. By all means, do that if that's what you're looking for and are able to afford it. Otherwise, know that there are other options where you don't have to pay and will also provide you with some sort of free accommodation and possibly a meal in exchange for a specific number of volunteer hours a week.

Examples of activities under this category that you can use to create content:

- Help maintain trails, sustainable eco-lodge, farms, etc.
- Help rescue animals
- Teach children
- Help create bicycle-powered energy
- Perform any volunteer activity organized through the Peace Corps

HEALTH & WELLNESS

Lastly, there are types of travel that allow you to expand your potential by focusing on wellness. Whether it is physical wellbeing, such as yoga, or a mental getaway, a spa retreat, etc., if this the type of travel that you are eventually seeking, there is an incredible variety of options.

Examples of activities under this category that you can use to create content:

- Learn or improve your skiing skills
- Discover the best ziplines
- Find nudist beaches. Or, find family-friendly beaches.
- Teach yoga or Ayurveda
- Sail
- Hike
- Climb

Types of Accommodations

Having an idea about the type of travel that you're looking to do as well as the budget that you have for it will help you determine the type of accommodation that you want and are able to pursue. There are many options available, even if your budget is limited. Let's determine which one is most suitable for you.

By the way, there are hundreds of resources available for you to find this information. The ones that I'm listing here are those that I researched and with which I'm more familiar, based on my years of experience traveling. In fact, I put a chart together to help you decide what your best option is based on your finances and the length of time that you're looking to stay in one specific place. Keep in mind that when I started my journey, my funds were very limited, so I enrolled in volunteer-based organizations, as that was all I could afford at that moment. Normally, a membership fee of around $50 is required and is good for one year. All I expected to do was to help out as a part-time volunteer (20-25 hours a week) in exchange for room and board. This is an amazing way to meet people from all over the world and, likely, friends with whom you'll keep in touch for a long time.

After endless nights of burning the midnight oil to meet unrealistic deadlines and sacrificing my time and life for the benefit of a corporation, I couldn't wait to meet volunteers from all over the world and share a relaxed meal around a bonfire. In fact, unless you have the means to stay at a hotel, international hostel, or even an AirBNB, you're likely to share space with other volunteers, possibly younger than you. Embrace it and enjoy a transformational moment. Not only will you be working with others towards a common goal, you'll also have the rest of the time to work on your own gig. This will be the core of your existence. The reason you spent so much time planning is for this moment right here, so that you can experience and gather the material you need to create the content that will help you monetize your passion.

For instance, after working a 4-hour shift at one of the volunteer places, you could take your camera and start documenting about the local lifestyle or do whatever project you are working on at the moment. You can then use that content and upload it to your website, YouTube channel, add it to your digital course, etc., which consequently would support your current and future trips in the manner explained previously on how to become a digital nomad. This moment right here is what it's all about - this is your chance to take it all in and learn about the world so that you can share it with others from your perspective.

If you are neither able to afford a hotel nor want to spend time volunteering, there are other options. Camping is a very economical way to travel and it would be a great solution if you are with someone else who loves camping as much as you do. I'm personally not sure if I would camp through places that are unknown to me by myself (even though I normally camp by myself in my home base) but of course, you need to do what makes you feel comfortable. Just remember that safety is first. There are also organizations such as Servas which has developed a worldwide hospitality network of more than 15,000 families and individuals in more than 100 countries in five continents. Their hosts are united by their desire to offer opportunities for goodwill visits, allowing for deeper, more personal contacts between people of diverse cultures and backgrounds from around the globe. However, the length of stay that they permit is usually a few days.

Remember that assessing the type of accommodation that you are able to afford does not mean you have to stick with it all the way through because you can always re-evaluate halfway and change your course.

Additionally, there are many possibilities when it comes to where to stay depending on how nomadic or sedentary you want your lifestyle to be. Maybe you are up for a combination of both? Some people like to stay in one place for one to three months and then move to another destination and so on. Isn't life wonderful and freeing when you can choose how long to stay in a place? I'm pretty sure that you are reading this because you dig the sense of adventure that exploring the world brings. If you're unsure as to where to start looking for the right place for you, this chapter will give you the guidance you need so that you can make the right decision. Or at least, point you in the right direction so that you get the hang of things. Trust me, the more time you spend on the road the better you'll get at finding the perfect accommodation to suit your needs. Here's a chart that will help you determine your best options:

Accomodations Based on Pricing

TYPE	DESCRIPTION	EXAMPLE	WEBSITE	LENGTH OF STAY	PRICE RANGE
HOTELS	Commercial hotels.	Any	Varies	Any	$$-$$$$$
HOSTELS	Lower-priced, sociable accommodations where guests can rent a bed in a dormitory and share a bathroom, lounge and a kitchen. Private rooms may also be available.	Hostel World	www.hostelworld.com	Up to 2 weeks	$-$$$$
		Hostelling International	www.hihostels.com	No more than 30 days	$-$$
BROKERS	Online marketplaces for arranging or offering lodging. These companies do not own any of the real estate listings. They act as brokers, receiving commissions from each booking.	AirBNB	www.airbnb.com	Varies	$-$$$
		9Flats	www.9flats.com	Varies	$-$$$
CAMPING OUT	Camp anywhere in the world.	Campspace	www.campspace.com	Varies	$
HOSTING (THROUGH AN ORGANIZATION)	Worldwide hospitality network in more than 100 countries. It allos for more personal contacts between people of diverse cultures and backgrounds from around the globe.	Servas	www.servas.org	1-3 days	FREE
HOSTING (BY INDIVIDUALS)	Homestay and social networking service accessible via a website and mobile app. The platform is a gift economy; hosts are not allowed to charge for lodging.	Couchsurfing	www.couchsurfing.com	1-7 days	FREE
FULL-TIME VOLUNTEER (FARMING)	Worldwide movement linking volunteers with organic farmers to promote cultural experiences thereby helping to build a sustainable, global community.	WWOOF	www.wwoof.org	Varies	FREE
PART-TIME VOLUNTEER (VARIED WORK)	Platforms that connect members with business owners so that they can arrange homestays and cultural exchanges for part time volunteer work.	Work Away	www.workaway.info	Varies but there's usually a minimum, not a maximum	FREE
		World Packers	www.worldpackers.com		
HOUSE OR PET SITTING	Connects pet and/or home owners with travelers. This platform allows individuals or couples to house or pet sit for the needed time.	Trusted House Sitters	www.trusted housesitters.com	Varies but there's usually a minimum, not a maximum	FREE

Table 13

AUDIO/BOOK RECOMMENDATION: If you're looking for pure inspiration on where to go and what to do, check the book 100 Best Worldwide Vacations to Enrich Your Life by Pam Grout.

TASK 9.1

Based on your budget and also based on the passion that you want to follow and monetize on, identify the type of travel that you want to do. Additionally, start the process of researching the type of accommodations that you are looking to secure. More details about Work Away and World Packers on Step 16.

STEP 10

Review Travel Documents

By now, you should have a pretty good idea about which country or countries you're going to visit based on the type of travel and accommodations that you are willing to pursue, but mostly based on the content you want to develop. In this step, we're going to look at all the general documents that you need in order to travel, but we'll also look at country-specific requirements, such as visas.

There are many documents that you want to ensure are up-to-date and have a validity of a few months, if not years, past the date that you are expected to return to home base. Arguably, none of them are as important as your passport.

However, all of the documents listed here are worth researching, whether it is for you to update or assess whether it's one for which you need to apply.

A passport is an official document issued by a government certifying the holder's identity and citizenship and entitling them to travel under its protection to and from foreign countries. A lot of countries will require that your passport doesn't expire for at least 6 months from the time you enter. Additionally, most countries will stamp your passport on the way in, and some will stamp it on the way out. Maybe you will travel to several countries and, because of this, you want to ensure that you have enough pages in your passport to withhold the test of time... and stamps.

A regular US passport book, for example, has a blue cover and is issued with the standard 28 pages and has a validity of 10 years. The validity of most countries' passports is 10 years, but their colors and number of pages will vary. There are many places where you can obtain or renew a passport, and the best source for accurate information is www.travel.state.gov. It normally takes between 6 to 8 weeks for the process to be completed, or you can pay extra and have your passport expedited in up to 3 weeks. Start by checking the expiration date on your passport. Many countries require at least six months' validity; otherwise, they reserve the right to deny you entry. If you do have to renew, make sure that you do so with plenty of time given the time frames mentioned.

Secondly, whether you're obtaining a passport for the first time or renewing yours, I would strongly recommend upgrading to a 52 page-passport (available for US passports) as there is no additional cost to do so. Especially if you are planning on traveling to several countries in short periods of time, the pages of your passport will get filled quickly and you certainly want to avoid renewing it from abroad. Even more so, if you already have visas imprinted in it, as visas from your old passport do not roll over, you'll want to avoid having to re-apply and pay for them again. Hopefully you will never need this piece of advice, but in case you do, if you ever lose your passport while travelling abroad, contact the nearest embassy or consulate of your country right away.

If you are a US citizen, you'll need to fill out Form DS-64, which is a statement regarding a lost or stolen passport. Then you'll have to fill out another form, DS-11, so you can apply for a replacement. If you are not a US citizen, familiarize yourself with the correct form or, at minimum, the appropriate process for passport replacement. This process will go smoother if you are able to provide a copy of your lost passport. This is why I recommend scanning a copy of it before you start your trip and emailing it to yourself for easy access. I personally always carry two passport photos with me in my travel folio. If I ever lose my passport and am in a country where I don't speak the language, I know that I will be able to get a replacement at the embassy much quicker if I'm able to provide them with a photo and with a copy of the lost passport.

As I mentioned earlier, remember to update your passport before applying for any visas. Some visas are glued or stamped onto your passport and they don't rollover or transfer to the new passport, unfortunately. Speaking of which, what exactly is a visa? A visa is an endorsement indicating that the holder is allowed to enter and stay for a specified period of time in a country. Whether you need a visa or not will depend on your country of citizenship, your country of residency in some instances, and most certainly the country(ies) to which you are travelling. You can check whether you need a visa or not by going to the official government travel website

https://travel.state.gov/content/travel/en/international-travel/ if you are a US citizen or, alternatively, to www.iatatravelcentre.com if you're not.

There are generally two types of tourist-related documents that will allow you to stay in a given country for a given period of time: a travel or tourist visa, and a tourist card. A travel or tourist visa is a formal request that you apply for ahead of time. Usually, you have to submit your active passport and mail it to the closest consulate of the country for which you wish to obtain a visa. For example, when I lived in Cincinnati, Ohio, the closest Brazilian consulate was in Chicago; therefore, I had to mail my US passport to Chicago along with a personal check, in order to obtain a Brazilian visa. This was 10 years ago. Most recently, I was able to do this online (e-Visa) and obtain the electronic version of the visa I was looking for. Luckily, now US citizens no longer need a visa to go to Brazil as tourists. There are other countries that will let you obtain a tourist card, which is just permission to enter as a tourist for a short period of time (just like a visa) but it's obtained at the target airport upon arrival to the country in question. For example, when I went to Paraguay in October of 2018, I didn't need to obtain a visa in advance, but when I landed at the Asunción airport, I was required to pay USD $160 for a tourist card that would allow me to stay for no more than 6 months at a time. This was, by far, the most expensive tourist card that I've ever had.

Also, when you cross the border into some countries, a customs agent will give you a form called an Entry Card. Do not lose it as it must be presented upon your departure. It can only be replaced at the offices of the local international police by showing your passport. If you are in a rush to get on a plane, by the time a replacement card is furnished to you, your flight would be long gone. Don't be that person!

Here is a document that I'm glad I applied for - the Global Entry - which includes the TSA PreCheck card. What are they and what's the difference between them? They are both part of the Trusted Traveler Program. TSA (or Transportation Security Administration) PreCheck allows you to skip the regular line and speed up the process to get to your gate by not requiring you to take your shoes off or take your laptop and liquids out as you go through security. The line is a lot shorter and moves a lot quicker. Global Entry allows you to skip the long line to come back into the US by speeding up the process through facial and digital recognition as set up on special kiosks in strategic places of the airport. TSA PreCheck is included with the Global Entry program but not vice versa. If you just have TSA PreCheck, it does not mean that you have Global Entry. Therefore, I would strongly recommend spending the additional fee and get Global Entry as it covers both programs. Additionally, as of March of 2020, 11 countries were added to the enrollment eligibility for Global Entry. Check eligibility here www.cbp.gov/travel/trusted-traveler-programs/global-entry

These programs originally started back in the 90's under a different name, but it was only available to frequent travelers who had a long history of mileage accumulated under their frequent flyer number from a given airline. It would then allow homeland security to speed up the security process, thus saving the government and airports millions of dollars annually. It was first available at airports in New York, Houston, and Washington DC. Then its success and effectiveness made sense and it expanded to more airports as well as to regular travelers who had to go through a strict screening process that included a background check and fingerprints.

US citizens and lawful US residents that qualify for the Global Entry and the TSA PreCheck program must be able to provide biographic information such as fingerprints, and criminal offenses will disqualify the applicant. The cost for the TSA PreCheck program is $85, which is a non-refundable fee, and the membership lasts for 5 years. The fee for Global Entry is $100, also non-refundable, and its membership also lasts for 5 years. This is a much better deal since with Global Entry you are expediting both the process to get to your gate and the process to get through customs and back to the US. There are two websites that will provide information and an application link: the TSA PreCheck website www.tsa.gov/precheck (that will only allow you to apply for TSA PreCheck) and the Global Entry website, where you'll be given the option of Global Entry and TSA PreCheck. My advice, just do Global Entry. There is also a related website www.ttp.dhs.gov which will give you additional documentation choices depending on where you travel more frequently. For instance, you could apply for the Sentri if you travel frequently to or from Mexico and the US; or for the Nexus if you travel to or from Canada on a regular basis.

As far as the process goes, first you submit the application online, then you schedule an interview near you in any of the available offices. Make sure that you show up on time and are well dressed. They will take your fingerprints and they will ask you a few biographic questions, that's all. Once you obtain your Global Entry card, it is important to confirm that your trusted traveler number appears on your boarding pass. If your trusted traveler number does not appear on your boarding pass, you don't get any of the benefits even if you show them your card. It happened to me when I most needed an expedited treatment, which obviously I didn't have.

Unfortunately, because of this mishap, I missed my flight. It was certainly nobody's fault but mine because I overslept (a traveler's worst nightmare), but I didn't know that I had to ensure that my trusted traveler number had to appear on the boarding pass either. To avoid this, ensure that your trusted traveler number is not only recorded with all the airlines for which you have a frequent flyer number, but also, when you book any flight, ensure that you confirm that number on your boarding pass, whether it's a print out or a digital version. If you're making the reservation over the phone with a live agent, let them know that you want to make sure that the TSA PreCheck symbol appears on the boarding pass.

Don't forget to update your Global Entry (or just TSA PreCheck) information in person in one of the designated offices should you update your passport. Your passport number changes when you update your document and the Global Entry and TSA PreCheck platforms are driven by your passport number, which doesn't change automatically.

TASK 10.1

Make sure that your passport is up to date, that you have plenty of time before it expires, and that you have enough empty pages for all of those visas, entry stamps, and exit stamps that it'll go through during your gap year. If not, make sure to renew it but ask for the 52-page version. Do so before applying for any visas (if applicable).

TASK 10.2

If you think you'll be traveling frequently enough to warrant applying for a Global Entry card, then do so. It saves so much time and it's just nice to be able to avoid those long lines, both going out and coming in.

STEP 11

Get the Necessary Vaccines

Vaccines can protect travelers from serious diseases. Depending on where you travel, you may come into contact with diseases that are rare in your region, such as yellow fever or malaria and for which we have not naturally built antibodies. There are vaccines that are "recommended" and there are vaccines that are "required". There are many places where you can check whether you need a vaccine or not, but my go-to websites are www.cdc.gov, the official US travel website www.travel.state.gov/content/travel/en/international-travel, or www.passporthealthusa.com. If you live outside the US, your best resource will be the International Society of Travel Medicine at www.istm.org where you can find the Global

Travel Clinic directory for the nearest clinics based on your location. Getting vaccinated not only will help you stay safe and healthy while traveling, but it will also prevent you from spreading any diseases back home or wherever else you're traveling next.

Do rely on experts in your area such as Passport Health USA, if you live in the US. For the longest time, I was trying to avoid them because I thought they were just a private business trying to make money off of travelers like myself. The truth is, they are the largest leading provider of travel medicine, immunization, and health travel consultation services in North America with over 270 travel clinic locations. In fact, the CDC (Center for Disease Control) has them listed as one of their authorized centers to administer vaccinations for travelers. You do have to pay $70 for the consultation, which I think it's a little steep and is why I was trying to avoid them, but I realized that this was still cheaper for me than going to my doctor and asking them for a prescription for my yellow fever vaccine, which nobody can administer without a prescription. I'm actually glad I went to Passport Health USA; the health consultant was very knowledgeable, and she even recommended that I get a few vaccines at my local pharmacy because they were going to be cheaper than getting them through them. In general, I felt that they were very helpful in providing options for what I really needed.

Should you need vaccines, record them on an International Certificate of Vaccination certificate or Prophylaxis, which is the only formal documentation accepted in many developing countries, as a form to prove that you have been vaccinated. I bought mine on Amazon for $12. Read more about it directly from the source, the World Health Organization at www.who.int/ihr/ports_airports/icvp_note/en/

INTERNATIONAL CERTIFICATE OF VACCINATION OR PROPHYLAXIS
AS APPROVED BY
THE WORLD HEALTH ORGANIZATION

CERTIFICAT INTERNATIONAL DE VACCINATION OU DE PROPHYLAXIE
APPROUVÉ PAR
L'ORGANISATION MONDIALE DE LA SANTE

TRAVELER'S NAME–NOM DU VOYAGEUR

ADDRESS–ADRESSE   (Number–Numéro)   (Street–Rue)

(City–Ville)

(County–Département)   (State–Pays)

DEPARTMENT OF HEALTH AND HUMAN SERVICES
CENTERS FOR DISEASE CONTROL AND PREVENTION

CDC 731 (formerly PHS-731)   CR113730

Image 1: *International Certificate of Vaccination or Prophylaxis*

127

The vaccines that you'll need to get are really going to depend not only on which country you go to, but also, where in the country you are planning to go. For instance, if you go to Brazil, likely you will need a yellow fever vaccine; also, typhoid if you are adventurous about trying street food, but not if you'll stay in a hotel and eat hotel food the entire time. A rabies vaccine might be needed if you'll be visiting places near the amazon and are planning on playing with monkeys. Please keep in mind that these generalizations do not replace the research and advice of health professionals who can tell you what's definitely needed, as well as the up-to-date advisory from the Center for Disease Control and Prevention (CDC) or the World Health Organization (WHO).

The vaccines that I chose to get prior to my trip, plus the consultation, totaled about $990 dollars. From what I understand, vaccines are vastly more expensive in the US than in any other region. Some folks even go as far as waiting to arrive in Asia in order to get the recommended vaccines for a lot cheaper. I understand that you can also get the MMR for free in Colombia or pay $3 for the Yellow Fever vaccine in Peru. I am no health expert, but I would agree with those who advise against this practice. It takes 2 to 3 weeks for a vaccine to build antibodies in your organism. That is a lot of time to leave your body vulnerable to all the possible contagions in the regions where you need it the most.

These are all the vaccines I was advised to get for Latin America:

- Flu ($45)
- Hepatitis A ($250)
- Hepatitis B ($250)
- Rabies (I declined this one because it was $1,000)

- TDAP: Tetanus/Diphtheria/Pertussis ($90)
- Typhoid ($135)
- Yellow Fever ($225) *Required

Here is additional information about the above and other common vaccines that travelers are advised to obtain based on their destination. The costs listed are in US dollars and are based on the information provided by Passport Health USA as of 2021. Additionally, a few of the following are routine vaccinations recommended for all travelers regardless of their target region:

Coronavirus: as of the publishing of this revised 1st edition, there's not yet a clear universal consensus regarding what countries will require in terms of the COVID-19 vaccination. Currently, most countries require a PCR test certificate that shows that the traveler recently tested negative for coronavirus. Several global companies are working on a vaccination passport, also known as 'immunity passport', likely in the form of an app, designed to show that the traveler has been vaccinated against COVID-19.

Flu: everybody is at risk all over the world and its transmission is airborne. Get the vaccine if it's not already part of your yearly routine. It might be free through your local pharmacy, but most commonly, this vaccine runs at about $45*

You can get **Hep A** from contaminated food and water and is needed for most countries. The vaccine is given in two parts and lasts a lifetime with a booster after 10 years.

You can get **Hep B** from unprotected sex with someone who is infected. The virus can also be passed through a person's blood, saliva, semen, vaginal secretions, or by sharing needles. This vaccine is also given in two parts and lasts a lifetime with a booster after 10 years.

The **Japanese Encephalitis** vaccine is recommended for travelers in Asia who plan to spend at least a month in areas where there is incidence of this disease, or less than a month in rural areas. The vaccine lasts 12 months and a booster is needed after that. It's a 2-shot series and each shot costs roughly $390.

Malaria is a serious and sometimes fatal disease caused by a parasite that commonly infects mosquitoes, which feed on humans. There isn't an effective malaria vaccine (4 injections with low efficacy) so malaria pills are rather preferred. Travelers to certain Asian and African regions are encouraged to seek the advice of health professionals regarding pill schedules. They come in packs of 24 pills and the cost of each pack is about $125.

The Meningococcal Meningitis vaccine is recommended for minors but also for adults with additional risk factors. Transmission is airborne and also through direct contact. It requires just a single dose, but later boosters may be recommended. A single shot is about $180. *

Better known as MMR: Measles, Mumps, Rubella. Everybody should already have these vaccines, but if in doubt, or are looking for a booster, these run at $125 per shot and it's a 2-shot series. Transmission is airborne and through direct contact. Its protection lasts a lifetime if you get the vaccine again as an adult. *

The Pneumococcal Pneumonia vaccine is recommended especially for those with certain medical conditions or who are immunocompromised. Transmission is airborne. This is a two-shot combo which, altogether, costs about $300. *

Poliomyelitis (better known as Polio) vaccine has been given to all children in the US since 2000 and it protects most (99 out of 100) who get all the recommended doses. For travelers, a single lifetime booster is recommended for certain countries. Transmission is through food and water. The cost is around $90. *

Rabies vaccines are given to people who are at a higher risk of coming into contact with animals with rabies. This vaccine is recommended if you're traveling to Asia or if you're going to a jungle where there are monkeys and bats, such as the Amazon. It's a 3-shot series, each shot costs $425, and it lasts for 3 years.

Shingles. Anyone who's had Chicken Pox (Varicella) may develop shingles and it's unknown what reactivates the virus. On one hand, the CDC recommends that healthy adults get two doses of the vaccine (separate by 2 to 6 months), but on the other hand, they advise not to get this vaccine if you have a weakened immune system or are getting cancer treatment. The cost is $250 per shot. *

TDAP: **Tetanus/Diphtheria/Pertussis.** Pertussis and tetanus are seen in all countries; diphtheria is more prevalent in Africa, India, Venezuela, Haiti, South East Asia. Transmission is airborne and through spores. The vaccine costs $90 and it lasts 10 years. *

The **Typhoid** vaccine is also recommended for most countries, especially in Southeast Asia, Africa, and rural Latin America. The form of transmission is via food and water. Typhoid pills are taken orally over the course of four doses and

131

provide protection for up to 5 years. The injection, on the other hand, is a one-time shot which offers protection for up to 2 years and the cost is about $135.

Everyone should have the **Varicella** (Chickenpox) vaccine. You should get it if you haven't received it already and have not been sick with chickenpox. It's a 2-shot series and the cost is $200 per shot. Transmission is airborne and also through direct contact. *

The **Yellow Fever** vaccine is required in a few countries and recommended in most countries in the Middle East, Asia, Africa, and South America. It costs about $225 and it lasts a lifetime.

*Routine vaccinations recommended for all travelers.

Opinions about vaccines not being required (such as Yellow Fever) are so varied and polarized that sometimes it's difficult to make up one's mind as to whether to get them or not. If this helps, consider that some travel insurances with medical riders won't cover treatment if you can't prove that you have been vaccinated against a specific ailment. In Step 18, we'll talk all about travel medical insurance, but right now, start researching about the vaccines that you will need because some of them come in a 2 or 3-part series. For example, the Hep A and Hep B vaccine is a 3-part combo and the first and third shot have to be administered 6 months apart. Plan accordingly!

This is a very helpful site that I sometimes refer to if I'm unsure of whether I should get a vaccine or not: www.travelhealthpro.org.uk/outbreaks and of course the CDC section of their website dedicated just to travelers wwwnc.cdc.gov/travel/

Don't forget bug repellent for dengue fever in tropical and subtropical areas; bug repellent for zika virus in all of the Americas except for Canada and Chile; and diarrhea pills for Asia, Africa, and Latin America due to virus, bacteria, and parasites. The latter is not glamorous, but the reality is that 70% of travelers are affected by traveler's diarrhea. Symptoms typically last 3 to 5 days or longer and life-threatening dehydration can occur in severe cases. This is why it is recommendable to only choose safe food and beverages, and depending on where you go, ask for bottled water. Avoid ice, as it's likely going to be made with tap water, and when they bring the water bottle to you, ensure that it's still sealed.

TASK 11.1

If you know for sure that you will need a Yellow Fever vaccine, then make an appointment with your Passport Health USA or equivalent travel consultant in your country of residency. If you do not need a Yellow Fever vaccine, then get the vaccines you need from your local pharmacy. Consulting your physician and getting a general checkup in preparation for your trip is always a good idea.

STEP 12

Start a Minimalistic Life

Back in Step 1 you started a comprehensive list of everything that composes your life, be that material things as well as intangible items such as bank accounts or internet subscription. Right now would be a good time to start taking action by selling what you can. You can do it yourself item by item, you can take it to a specialized store where they'd do this for you, or you can have someone else like a friend help you list the items on a selling platform and give them a portion of the sales. I experienced all three alternatives and here are my perspectives:

I first asked a friend to help me list the items on Facebook Marketplace. She took the pictures, wrote the title and description and I just responded to inquiries and met potential buyers to eventually sell the items. I gave her 15% of the sale just because she saved me so much time. It was worth it, but honestly, taking the pictures and listing it yourself doesn't take that long. I think that since it was my first experience with Facebook Marketplace, I was a little reluctant to learn how to do it at first. After many items sold, I started creating the listings myself so I didn't have to split my earnings. Though honestly, I would much rather share the wealth with a friend. It's a lot more fun than doing all the work alone. The only hassle was to deal with all the inquiries and potential buyers because it's time consuming.

A couple of years ago, I had started a t-shirt business with the intention of leaving someone I trusted to manage it for me. I was going to split half of the profit, which I thought was a generous offer. However, a few months prior to my trip, this person informed me that he had no time to help me manage the business because he had a busy schedule. Well, it would have been nice to know that in advance as I could have trained someone else for the task. I didn't want to delay my departure date so, at that point, it was going to be easier for me to get rid of the gig altogether. For the sake of minimalism, it would be one less thing that I had to worry about from the faraway lands. I then sold it as an incorporated turnkey business. A few of the machines I sold separately, and I was able to list them on Facebook Marketplace. Including these items, a heat press and a vinyl cutter, as well as the rest of the items I sold (not including the business itself), I probably made close to $4,000 (the heat press alone was $1,800). I know I could have sold more items should I have had the time for it. That's when I turned to consignment deals.

After having worked in the corporate world for over 20 years, I had accumulated a decent number of really good brand name clothes and shoes. Half of them were new since I made sure I always wore the latest and greatest. I would spend a little bit at the end of each quarter, right after our awaited bonus. However, all of that stopped when I decided to travel full time and to become a minimalist instead. I'm almost ashamed to admit that I needed 2 closets to gather all of my precious belongings. I took 90% of those items to a local consignment store to be sold. Be mindful that these stores will usually take items that are right for the season. This means that you might be sent home with items that they still will want, but not just yet.

Taking items to a consignment shop was probably a lot easier than dealing with selling each item myself separately, but because of that, I didn't make as much money. I think that probably altogether I made not quite $200, even though clothes and shoes were high quality and in great condition. That probably paid for one of the vaccines I had to have. The truth is, I felt so light after getting rid of most of my clothes and shoes. It's a feeling of generalized freedom and difficult to explain unless you go through it yourself. Seeing how each room of my home was becoming emptier and emptier was somehow exhilarating. I remember wishing I would have become a minimalist a lot sooner.

Something important to consider is to leave a few pieces of clothes and shoes behind in case you have to come back to your home base for a job interview, an emergency, a wedding, a funeral, or any other type of unexpected event. You could keep these in storage or at a friend's place. This should be part of your exit strategy as explained in the next step, in case you're keeping a list in your travel-planning notebook.

Everything that you cannot sell, donate it or give it away. If you donate it to a non-profit organization, get a receipt for tax purposes. Feel free to reference Step 5 regarding tax deductions on donations for a reminder of why this is important. There will be things that you may have to either replace or leave as is. When I decided to embark on this journey, I worked hard to pay my house off and decided that I needed to rent it out because of monetary family obligations. My property manager inquired if I could leave the furniture because a furnished home was apparently more appealing for corporate tenants. I was happy to do so because the furniture I had was in good condition, but rather old. Not having to deal with moving it out of the house was an absolute win-win. However, I had to make sure that I replaced the gas range stove and fix a few other items. All of these things were in my sub-category list #2, Start a Minimalistic Life (created from Step 1), otherwise, I likely would not have remembered to address these items until the last minute.

Do a little bit at a time so as not to get overwhelmed or dedicate an entire week for this project and get it over with. It's completely up to you, and don't forget to have fun in the process!

AUDIO/BOOK RECOMMENDATION: I think that by now, most people have heard of the book about minimalism. This is hands down the best book I could possibly recommend about this topic: Essential: Essays by the Minimalists by Joshua Fields Millburn and Ryan Nicodemus. To quote just one of their many valuable lessons, if you can get rid of everything and avoid storing, do it. If you can't, well, you have to do what's right for you. I can tell you from personal experience that letting go of things is not easy at all, but it's very liberating when it happens. We put so much emotion into memories and to the feelings they give us that getting rid of that it is very hard. I get it. I invite you to try baby steps and part with the most you can for the sake of building a new you.

TASK 12.1

Pull out your main list and transfer items from that list to this sub-list. Start selling, donating, giving away, and replacing. Towards the very end, throw away what you can and store what you absolutely have to.

Sub-List From Step 1 (2) **Start a Minimalistic Life**
a. Sell
b. Donate (ask for a tax receipt)
c. Give away or throw away
d. Leave as is
e. Replace
f. Store

Section 2 of Table 5

STEP 13

Design an Exit Strategy

Just like in poker and stock trading, in most aspects of life, it is pivotal to know not only when to fold, but also how to fold, meaning, when and how to walk away. This type of planning is what makes the difference between a successful player (stock trader, world traveler, etc.) and an unprepared one. An exit strategy may look different for everyone, but regardless, money and finances are going to play a big role in it.

Your exit strategy will also depend on how long you're planning on being away, but if you don't yet have an idea on how long that will be or you're leaving that aspect open-ended, you definitely want to assess all of the aspects of your life as you did in Step 1 and ask yourself how you can bring that part of your life back, should you need to. A car would be a great example to illustrate this. If you think you'll be gone for at least a couple of years, chances are you will not want to spend money on monthly car insurance, a car payment, regular maintenance, possibly a storage fee, or just burden someone to take care of it. In which case, selling your car might be the best solution because it will not only save you money, but it will also be one less thing that you'll need to worry about. The fewer things you have on your radar to worry about while abroad, the better.

So, you sold the car right before leaving to go on your worldly adventure. Now you're back and need a means of transportation. Think of the worst and the best-case scenario. Your best-case scenario is that you made a great living abroad and profited enough that you are able to buy whatever vehicle you want, at least in the price range available. The worst-case scenario is coming back with no money at all. What do you do then? Probably the best plan is to stash aside enough money to purchase an economical vehicle while you get back on track. The dollar amount that you allocate will depend on the state in which you live. But don't leave for your trip unless you have saved enough in your emergency bucket for that just-in-case car, should you need to be back before you had planned, or simply for your scheduled return.

If you rent an apartment and give it up, no big deal. Just look for another one, but make sure that you have at least three months-worth of rent (and the security deposit) saved up. If you own your home but are renting it out, give notice to the property administrator as soon as possible, but plan on renting a temporary space, as you might not be able to move back if the tenants have signed a long-term lease. To minimize risks, when you leave, have the property manager set up your tenants with the shortest possible lease at first; that way, you can test the waters and see how you adapt to your new lifestyle before making it more permanent.

If you are leaving items in a storage facility, leave a suitcase with clothes for all seasons (summer, winter, and anything in between) and everything else that you might need for three months or until you get back on your feet. Definitely set clothes aside for job interviews, a funeral, or any other event such as a wedding. You can always buy clothes upon your return, unexpected or not, but if you are looking to do the frugal thing, then make sure to stash emergency outfits, one for each occasion.

Before you leave, make sure that you update your resume in case you need to start looking for a job earlier than planned. Updating your LinkedIn on a regular basis with stories about your travels is a great idea. Employers don't mind a gap in your work history if it can be explained with an amazing experience around the world. It provides an incredible edge and a great advantage over other candidates (depending on your line of work) as it provides a unique perspective; they will likely be looking forward to getting you on board their team so that you can spread all of that worldly knowledge onto them. Trust me, they will be fighting to hire you.

Most importantly, talk to your closest friends and maintain constant contact with them. Before you leave, explain that there might be a chance that you could return sooner than expected and ask them if you could crash at their place for a few days before you figure things out. Likely, this will not be necessary, but if it must happen, you don't want to catch them off guard. They will be happy to help a friend in need.

If it's a possibility, hide some cash in a safety box inside your storage unit or at a safety box at your bank (where nobody has digital access to), or with a friend. This will help you through the first week or so while you figure things out, should you be in a dire situation.

Contact your insurance company before you leave and keep them abreast of your plans. When you return, do the same so that they are aware and continue with whatever policies you need.

Sometimes, creating an exit strategy does not necessarily mean replacing material items or having the funds to survive for a few months upon your return. Sometimes, an exit strategy literally means to have a process when there is an emergency in the area that you're visiting. There are so many reasons why an evacuation could take place in any given area: terrorism, crime, natural disasters, a pandemic, or even a personal medical emergency. None of us have a way of knowing in advance what's going to happen, when, or where, but being part of a network that can guide you through should the unexpected occur is sometimes the best situation that you can be in.

Years ago, I enrolled in the STEP program, which is the Smart Traveler Enrollment Program. This is a free service to allow US citizens traveling abroad to enroll with the local US Embassy or Consulate. Every time I plan a trip, I go online and I specify the dates I'll be in each country, as well as my emergency contact. This is a very easy way for me to stay up to date on everything going on in real time because if something happens, the embassy and/or consulate will send daily communications to you via email and provide a status or further guidelines. This also works the other way. If there is an emergency at home and my family is not able to get a hold of me, they will reach out to the closest embassy, which will have the address of the hostel I'm staying at and they will attempt to reach me to get me in contact with my family. To enroll, simply go to www.step.state.gov

TASK 13.1

Think about those aspects that you will need to consider upon your return or if you have to get back sooner than expected for one reason or another: rent, a car, your updated resume, an emergency fund, clothing, etc. For example, set enough money aside to be able to buy the most expensive plane ticket from wherever you are to your home base, should an emergency come up. Your main list from Step 1 can be your best guide so that nothing falls through the cracks. The point is not to replace everything you got rid of before you embark on your trip, but rather, to get by comfortably until you find a more permanent situation.

TASK 13.2

If you're a US citizen, enroll in STEP (the Smart Traveler Enrollment Program) and keep your information up to date regarding the countries you'll be in, the address of where you'll be, and a couple of emergency contacts. If you're not a US citizen, find out if your government's consulate or embassy has a similar service. Before you arrive in each country, know where the nearest embassy or consulate is in case of an emergency.

Cancel Subscriptions and Memberships

From your master list from Step 1 (brain dump) you also created the following sub-list:

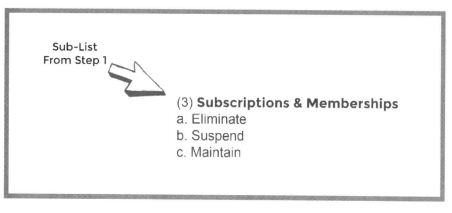

Sub-List
From Step 1

(3) **Subscriptions & Memberships**
a. Eliminate
b. Suspend
c. Maintain

Section 3 of Table 5

At this point, you should have a pretty good idea of what you will need to cancel and what you will need to suspend. With any membership, check in advance to understand what the process looks like and what the effective turnaround time is. For example, I called my gym to find out how to cancel my membership and they told me that I could cancel at any time, but the cancelation would become effective on the first day of the month following the cancellation. At the same time, they suggested suspending service instead, and I would only have to pay $5 a month. In comparison to the $200 initiation fee that I would have to pay should I decide to reinstate the membership when I come back, that's something that I will, at minimum, consider.

Go through all the items that you have on this list, call them, explain what you're looking to do, negotiate a lower fee while you're at it, and finally, either put it on your calendar to follow up on it as a suspension, or to cancel it altogether if that is a possibility.

If you decided to rent out your home while traveling, your property manager will likely recommend that you continue paying for water. I think that this is a very good piece of advice for many reasons. First, some areas require water to stay in the owners' name, so sometimes you don't have a choice. Second, this service is attached to the owner of the house and if tenants fail to pay for the water, after enough time, the city could place a lien against the property for the amount owed. Lastly, especially in wintertime, it's good to have control over the water supply. In that case, if there are no tenants living in the house, the property manager is able to keep the pipes running to avoid a freeze if temperatures fall dramatically. This, of course, only applies to folks who live in places that get freezing cold in the winter.

Also, by now, you may have already started your digital footprint in order to generate income while away. If so, there will be many subscriptions that you'll have to maintain, depending on your marketing venue of choice. For instance, if you went the blogger way (like most of us), you may have had to create a website. As such, you need to be on top of your domain expiration date, website services expiration date, and everything that comes with it. Regardless of what type of subscription you got yourself into, make sure that you keep a worksheet with all of your logins and remove two-way authentications, if at all possible.

Removing two-way authentications was a tough choice for me to make. After working 11 years in a very security-restricted environment (as the financial industry is) where we had to change our passwords every month. I'm big on cyber security to the point that I update my bank and financial-related passwords every quarter and I combine numbers, letters, symbols (if I can), and upper cases. I go all out. Well, not at the Edward Snowden level but I have two-way authentication on just about everything. My cell phone is usually the device I use to approve access to another device or to a bank account online, for example. However, since I'm planning on suspending my phone service before my trip, and in the event that one of my devices gets stolen, I don't want to deal with not being able to verify my identity as I try to convince customer service that it's really me and I need to get into my accounts pronto.

TASK 14.1

Try to be as minimalist as you possibly can and avoid more subscriptions than you have to. Have all of your passwords stored in a couple of safe places, encrypted, and password secure. Remove two-way identification (optional, personal choice). Contact all of the companies you subscribe to (i.e., phone carrier) to understand the process to unsubscribe, suspend, and reinstate. Write it all down in your notebook with the dates of which you spoke to their customer service in case you need to reference it.

Choose: Suitcase or Backpack?

I have to be honest here, I'm not sure I'm the most qualified individual to advise on anything related to packing. In fact, I'm the worst. I'm the type of person who, on a regular 10-day vacation, besides her carry-on and personal item, will check two bags and one of them would be full of shoes. No joke. There are people, on the other hand, that not only are able to pack in a very efficient and compact manner but are also able to go without a checked bag. How is that even possible? I'm the poster child for the 'just in case,' the 'you never know,' and the 'I'd feel better knowing that I have it,' type of person.

Unwantedly, I've been an overachiever all of my life because I tend to plan for the 10 steps ahead and, in this particular case, I carry with me all the elements I need for all the hundreds of possible scenarios that could occur. Yes, it is exhausting sometimes, exhilarating most of the time, fun to strategize about, amazing when I actually do need the 'just in case' item, but very inefficient when it comes to packing for a sabbatical year. It was not easy for me, but eventually I got it, and as follows is the summary of my own learnings.

Let's start with the type of suitcase or backpack needed. If you will stay in one or up to six places in one year, you might be able to get away with bringing a large suitcase and checking it. That's roughly one place every 2 months, on average. However, if you're planning on volunteering and staying in one place or more per month, then maybe a backpack might be a better choice. This is, of course, a very personal decision.

This reminds me of the time I went backpacking through Japan for two weeks many years ago. I took a backpack that someone had given to me as a Christmas gift which I hadn't used before that trip. This was a 65-liter backpack, and at that time, I knew nothing about backpack capacities and things like that. By the way, I'm barely 5'1" and my backpack was beyond full (in case there was any doubt) plus I was carrying another overpacked, regular-sized backpack in front of me. I'm not sure people could see me well - I probably looked like a vertical turtle struggling hard not to fall. It was rough, my back and shoulders hurt a lot and as soon as I returned from my trip, I went straight to REI for advice. They told me that a 65-liter backpack for someone my height and build was way too big, which made absolute sense. The REI employee was incredibly helpful, and I spent 45 minutes trying many backpacks with and without weight inside them to ensure that I was 100% satisfied and able to carry it for an extended period of time without breaking my back. They even made me walk with it inside the store for 5 minutes just to test things out.

The moral of the story is, the backpack that you choose is important and you should not take that decision lightly. Do your research on YouTube or go to an REI store if you have one available near you. Even if you don't buy anything, REI associates will be very helpful in explaining what you need to know to make the best decision. As a result, I got a 45-liter backpack, which extends to 50 liters, and it's very comfortable for me.

Speaking of REI, only if it makes sense for you, consider becoming a member. If your hiking boots or backpack breaks, you can order a replacement and they'll ship them to you anywhere you are in the world, except for Australia due to tax laws. They will ship internationally for only $20 if the order is less than $150 dollars or free if the order is over $150. That's an awesome deal if you ask me. Keep in mind however, that shipping takes longer, plus you are responsible for local duties and taxes. Depending on the country, this could get pricey the bigger the package is. Then again, you could always wait until you get to civilization and just buy whatever you need without the replacement warranty that REI offers.

Now, let's talk about what to bring along. In my case, I wanted to force myself to bring everything I was going to need in a year in my backpack and not even consider that I could also carry a small backpack with me. However, I did buy a small slinger bag which I carry in front of me so that I can have easy and quick access to my mirrorless camera, passport, wallet, phone, and immediate items. And this is the rest of my packing list:

THE PACKING LIST

of a DIGITAL NOMAD

Clothes

- o 1 balaclava
- o 1 baseball hat
- o 1 bathing suit
- o 1 down jacket/raincoat
- o 1 dress
- o 1 light hoodie
- o light scarf to cover my head
- o long hiking pants
- o long legs pajama
- o 1 pair of city sandals
- o 1 pair of city shorts
- o 1 pair of gloves
- o 1 pair of gym shorts
- o 1 pair of hiking shoes
- o 1 pair of running shoes
- o 1 pair of shower sandals
- o 1 pair of sweatpants
- o 1 pair of walking/hiking sandals
- o 1 short pajama
- o 1 sweater
- o 1 warm hat
- o 2 pairs of socks
- o 2 t-shirts
- o Regular glasses
- o Sunglasses
- o Undergarment

Documents

- o An extra passport photo ID
- o Copy of passport
- o Global Entry card
- o Home-based driver's license
- o International Driving Permit
- o Itinerary
- o Passport
- o Phone numbers printed on a sheet of paper
- o Vaccines certificate booklet

Electronics

- o Adaptors
- o Aux cable
- o Battery chargers
- o Cell phone
- o Charger cables
- o Computer
- o External portable hard drive (slim, 2T)
- o GoPro
- o HDMI cable
- o Headphones
- o Lapel microphone
- o Memory cards
- o Memory sticks
- o Mirrorless camera
- o Mouse
- o Small dry box for flash drives
- o Stainless steel credit card case for SIM cards
- o Tripod
- o Ultra-compact portable power bank
- o Various lenses

Survival

- o **Headlamp**
- o Portable hammock
- o Rope bracelet
- o Silicone flat large cup
- o Spork
- o Whistle

Toiletries

- o Body lotion
- o Bugspray
- o Comb
- o Conditioner
- o Deodorant
- o Face cream
- o Floss
- o Lip balm
- o Medium towel
- o Mucinex
- o Nail cutter
- o Prescription medicine
- o Q-tips
- o Shampoo
- o Soap
- o SPF 100 sports
- o Toothbrush
- o Toothpaste
- o Tweezers

Table 14

Lastly, having lost a very nice mirrorless camera a while back I am overly cautious about my electronics and expensive items. You may already know about Tile products, but if you've never heard of them, I would definitely recommend looking into them for your trip. These are very small devices that you attach to any of your material possessions and are able to track them via Bluetooth. They come in 4 different sizes and shapes, and pricing is mostly based on their respective reach. The smallest of them is called the 'Sticker', a round 1 x 1-inch device that you can glue to your camera, your tripod, your computer, or anything of value, but only has 150 feet reach. I bought mine on Amazon, although Apple has been trying to launch the equivalent, but up to the publishing date of this book, they have not done so. I found many brands of similar devices offering tracking, but I found Tile to have the best reviews, app support, and pricing. In fact, the Tile community is so increasingly strong that if one of your lost items is out of reach, people will communicate with you through the Community section of the app and help you find it if an item is marked as lost and it's near them (a sound is made when you mark it as 'lost'). Pretty cool, eh?

If Tiles are out of your budget, there are many other ways to secure your items. Always bring a combination lock along and a vigilante cable lock. NRS makes quality items and REI sells them online. They run for about $20 and it comes with a combination lock. I saw a backpacker once who had a wrist leash tied to his day pack, the type of leash that parents use with their toddlers. I thought that was a pretty good idea. The level of petty crime in other countries could be different than what you're used to. For instance, in Santiago, Chile or in Barcelona, Spain, pickpocketing is, unfortunately, very common. Just be alert and aware of your surroundings, protect your belongings, don't flash your phone or electronics. If you think it's appropriate, wear your day packs in front of you, not on your back. Don't ever leave your items unattended.

TASK 15.1

In Step 1 you created a sub-list for your Trip-Related items. Start gathering all those items that you are considering taking with you on your trip and pack them in your suitcase or backpack to ensure that they fit. I had to do this exercise several times and each time I had to remove a few items until I was able to keep it all in my backpack.

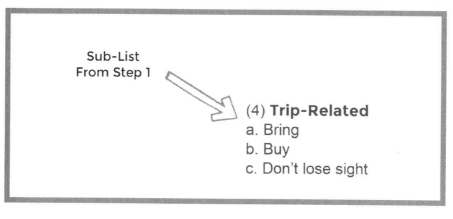

Section 4 of Table 5

Register for Work Away or World Packers

This is the part where we're drastically different from the rest of the terrestrials out there. Regardless of your age, wouldn't you much rather volunteer your time, hang out with a bunch of volunteers from all over the world, do good work that will have an impact on this good earth, AND receive room and board for free? I know I would. In fact, if it wasn't for this way of exchange, I don't think I could consider traveling the world since I'm on a tight budget. I don't think that most of us could, at least not at the beginning of that first gap year. The work that you're doing is so that you can take a year off, but the truth is that many of us can't stop after that. I know I won't be able to, and I will want to continue traveling. After you start to travel and if you are able to monetize on your gig right away, you'll encounter the decision of whether you want to upgrade and start traveling without having to volunteer or continue volunteering while pocketing your earnings. That's a great dilemma to be in, congratulations if you get there. If not, the volunteer life is still the best feeling ever.

Keep in mind that there are websites out there (i.e., Couchsurfing.com) that will let you crash on someone's couch for a few nights, expecting nothing in return. I have never couchsurfed, but I have talked to people who have and have had good experiences with these hosts. I have also read about horror stories. Above anything (more important than the money you save), be cautious, be alert, and be smart. For the time being, let's focus on the volunteer arrangements that will allow you to save north of $20,000, if you play it right. I've found several sites that will allow you to register and get connected with hosts from all over the world that will ask for 20-25 hours of volunteer work in exchange for room and board, or just board at minimum. The following sites are confirmed legit sites, you can find volunteer reviews, and once you register, you can even reach out to the volunteers who have worked for these hosts in the past and ask them specific questions.

The websites that I have discovered so far are these:

1. WorkAway.info
2. WorldPackers.com
3. TrustedHouseSitters.com

It's worth noting that a work visa is not required because you aren't working in exchange for money, but rather, are doing volunteer work in exchange for room and board.

However, if you want to pursue temporary work in one of the countries you're going to, maybe look into obtaining a temporary holiday work visa, though keep in mind that not all countries offer it. If they do, they may restrict the citizenship of the applicants that they approve. Their respective embassy or consulate website might be the best source for this information.

WorkAway.info and WorldPackers.com are platforms that allow members to arrange homestays and cultural exchange. Volunteers are expected to contribute a pre-agreed amount of time per day or per week in exchange for lodging and food, which is provided by their host. There are over 40,000 hosts registered in over 170 countries. The price is about $42 yearly to register as a single volunteer, though it's possible to register and volunteer as a couple. Part of that amount that you pay gets donated to the Work Away Foundation. Depending on the host and the type of work expected, the minimum number of weeks expected of a volunteer as a commitment is 2 weeks. Also, there are a lot of hosts out there looking for a long-term commitment of up to a year. The type of job is agreed upon in advance and both hosts and volunteers get the opportunity to rate each other once the work commitment is finished.

WorldPackers.com is a platform which connects travelers looking to exchange their skills for accommodation with hosts from all over the world. The yearly membership costs $49 and it works just like WorkAway.info. And just like its counterpart, this is a great way to see the world on a budget; it's safe because hosts are not only registered in this platform and have to go through a screening process, but also have to post photos of themselves on their profiles and reviews can be written about them, and about the volunteers as well.

161

TrustedHouseSitters.com is where you can find thousands of housesitting or pet-sitting opportunities. The membership costs about $129 a year for unlimited sits. They've been in business for 9 years and they have glorious reviews. According to their website, there are no specific qualifications needed to become a sitter, but when first starting out (before you are able to obtain reviews), getting a reference from someone who knows you, for whom you have pet or house sat, or has seen you hold a position of responsibility, might help you get your first gigs. I have personally not applied for this type of work yet, but I requested a reference letter to the parents of my favorite doggo, Mango, who I adore, and pet sit as often as I can. I keep that letter digitally, along with pictures of Mango and I, in case I decide to apply for a sweet house or pet sitting gig along the way.

Even though I will soon start my nomadic life, so far, I have had great experience with WorkAway.info and also with WorldPackers.com. I've been able to connect with many hosts, who seem as eager to meet me than I am to meet them. I've also been able to connect with volunteers who have stayed with the hosts I've applied to, just to get their thoughts. I have not utilized TrustedHouseSitters.com yet, but it seems to be very legit as well. One piece of advice is to be open to learning new things - meeting people from all over the planet who may have different perspectives than yours. I personally try to go the extra mile because that goes a long way. Besides, remember that both hosts and volunteers review each other at the end of each stay. This review is public within each platform and, the better the review, the more you ensure that other hosts will choose you over other applicants. Always keep a positive attitude, offer a lending hand, even if it's not in your job description, and do your best to get along with everyone.

Before registering for these two sites, I wrote down the countries I wanted to visit and the month I wanted to be there just to have an idea of the type of volunteer work I wanted to commit to. Specifically, during my first year I wanted to visit South America only. I researched the best times of the year to be in each country, and, along with each geographical location, I was able to align all the countries I wanted to visit, as well as the length of time I wanted to spend in each. At first, I reached out to a few hosts, but only one of them responded. That's normal, don't freak out. It seems like many of them arrange last minute work and I was trying to set everything up too early in advance. I reached out in February to arrange work for August. Apparently, things don't work like that in those 'necks of the woods' and I should have known that, since I am originally from Latin America. I was able to arrange my first three months of travel, but I was going to depart not having my entire year planned out, which was so outside of my comfort zone. However, I had decided that one way or another, everything was going to work out and that was that.

TASK 16.1

Gather 6 to 10 of your best pictures where you appear with friends on vacation, having fun and preferably enjoying your hobbies. Register to volunteer by creating your profile and paying your membership. World Packers encourages you to create a 2-minute video and post it privately on YouTube so that you can introduce yourself to your potential hosts. This is a great idea because they are able to see your personality, which is difficult to convey in pictures. Start reaching out to all of the possible places you want to visit. Sort hosts by the type of work offered, based on what you're able and willing to do. For example, I love the outdoors but I'm sometimes allergic to a few plants. Farming was out of the question for me. Instead, I'd apply for other type of gigs such as bartending or even animal care. Apply to many because not all of the ones you write to will reply back. Be flexible, courteous, and keep your options open.

STEP 17

Write Up A Living Will and a Last Will

This topic is by no means intended to be morbid or to make you feel uncomfortable. The truth is that we are all going to leave this earth one way or another and there is nothing that you or I can do about it. Well, there is one thing that you could do about it and that's the topic of this section. It may help you to think about this if we imagine the unimaginable and think about how to start collecting estate planning information about a close relative's assets, should they pass. Do you know their bank account information, real estate information, named executor, or even medical power of attorney if they are in a vegetative state? Very likely, most people would answer "no" to the above. Now, imagine how much easier things would be for your relatives if you leave all the necessary instructions should something happen to you while traveling abroad. Of course, nothing will happen, but at least you'll know that your loved ones will have the peace of mind when they need it most.

What is the difference between a living will and a final testament? Do you need pre-need insurance? Do you need to go through all of this if you don't have assets? I am not qualified to provide a professional answer, so I'll defer you to your attorney or tax advisor to get the answers to all of your questions on the matter. However, I've written this chapter because I do believe that it is important to leave some sort of instructions before you embark on your travels and assign somebody close to you (as well as a backup person) with enough power to:

- Follow your instructions in a living will or medical power of attorney in case you are not able to make your own medical decisions.
- Make your relatives aware that you have left a last testament.

What is a living will? This is an excerpt from alllaw.com: "A living will, also called a directive to physicians or advance directive, is a document that lets people state their wishes for end-of-life medical care, in case they become unable to communicate their decisions. It has no power after death." I have personally used a living will to list all of my bank accounts and important information, just in case. In that way, I use one document for two purposes: as a medical directive, but also to make things easier for my family, should something happen to me. As a result, not only will they know how to proceed, but they will also know what assets there are, even if they are not able to access them until after I pass. Remember, a living will only provide medical instructions to whomever you specify. I'm adding a list of my assets so that my relatives become aware of what's in my name, not because they'll be able to take any action. My last testament and will, on the other hand, is what allows an executor (whoever I name) to divide the assets in the way I specify.

What is a will or last testament? The following is an excerpt from Fidelity.com, from the Planning section: "A will and last testament is a legal document that clarifies how and to whom the deceased's assets are to be distributed. It usually includes:

- Designation of an executor, who carries out the will.
- Beneficiaries—those who are inheriting the assets.
- How and when the beneficiaries will receive the assets.

Assets passing in the will must undergo the probate process. Probate is the process of settling your estate according to your will."

Also, consider getting Pre-Need insurance before you leave. The truth is, everybody should have some type of life insurance and pre-need insurance as well. I worked for two years for a pre-need insurance company, so I think I can answer this question with certainty, though I will still quote an excerpt from www.policygenius.com which states that: "Pre-need insurance is used to pay for the costs of funeral services and burial or cremation. What's unusual about pre-need plans compared to other types of insurance is that you work directly with a funeral home. They'll price expenses — cemetery plot, services, casket, burial, etc. — and your insurance policy covers those costs. The beneficiary of a pre-need insurance policy is the funeral home. They'll receive the money to pay for their services."

The two main benefits of having pre-need insurance is that your relatives will not have to go through the pain of choosing the casket or paying for funeral costs. Maybe you wish to be cremated? Any services that you want to specify and add to your pre-need policy will be performed by the funeral home that you assign. The price is guaranteed and it's very regulated so there are no surprises for your survivors.

However, and regardless of what you choose to do, it is always a good idea to assign beneficiaries to all of your accounts, provide written instructions to at least two people regarding medical situations, and to settle all of your matters before you go on your world tour. You will be glad you did!

TASK 17.1

Consult with a lawyer on what the next steps are to draft up a living will and also a last testament. If you, like myself, are on a budget and are looking to save on legal fees, check websites that can provide templates and a way to do it yourself in a legit manner. I recommend www.willing.com because you can also register your last testament through your state (if you are a US resident).

STEP 18

Research Travel Medical Insurance

Whether you are traveling for a few months, for a year, or more you may want to consider keeping your health insurance. It might be confusing for some, as the initial thought is to replace health insurance for traveler medical insurance (travel insurance with a medical rider). They are both completely different, yet they complement each other. For example, if you are traveling and get sick, you can use your travel medical insurance at most places to see a doctor and get medicine, or even to be hospitalized, up to a certain amount. However, if you fall severely ill and need surgery or major treatment, your travel medical insurance will likely not cover these expenses. Travel medical insurance, in this case, is used to evacuate you and get you back home where you can get appropriate care by using your regular health insurance.

Travel medical insurance does not replace your regular health insurance as they both cover different angles (for the most part). However, many of these angles may overlap. In fact, the lines where both intertwine are so gray that it will be your job to discern these differences before making a final decision on which type of travel insurance to purchase. But no worries, I'll walk you through. By the way, when you start researching this online, you'll notice that people use different terms (travel insurance, trip insurance, traveler medical insurance, travel health insurance, and many more) to mean the same thing: the type of insurance you get that will cover your travel-related mishaps, whether they be airfare, equipment, or health related. How much of each of these categories will your insurance cover? It will depend on the company you end up hiring for the task along with the package you select, which, in turn, will depend on what you need.

Let's start with trip insurance. This type of insurance could cover things like flight cancellation and interruption, whether it is caused by the airline, weather, or if something came up where can't make the flight. It also covers baggage and belongings, in case the airline loses your items or if they are stolen at a hostel...things like that. Be very careful of the dollar amount that you're specifying for both case scenarios, baggage claim and stolen items. When you buy trip insurance at the same time that you're buying your airfare, the default cap on baggage claim is usually $300-$500. The higher the number, the more expensive the policy becomes. Make sure that you're covered. The right travel health insurance will depend on your personal situation. The trick is to find the balance to not overpay, but also not leave yourself without coverage. The first thing that I would recommend is contacting your current health insurance and have them send you a written summary of what's covered by them while you're traveling abroad. All plans are going to be very different from each other, so you need to understand how your current health insurance works and what it does and does not cover while you're traveling outside your country from a medical perspective. You want to make sure to have this in writing. Let me share my experience so that you can understand the good, the bad, and the ugly.

Years ago, I had amazing health benefits when I worked at Fidelity Investments. I once went skiing during my vacation time in Chile. I fell on my way down one of the slopes and hurt my knee -and my ego- very badly, went to the emergency room, got my knee treated, and I even started pre-diabetic treatment with a nutritionist there as the doctor in the emergency room realized that my fall was due to abnormal levels of glucose in my bloodstream. When I got back home, I filled out a claim through work and my health insurance covered everything. Everything. Granted, it was only a month-long vacation, but the bottom line is that I did not need travelers' medical insurance because my regular health insurance at that time was so robust that it covered what I needed it to cover.

On the opposite side of the spectrum is my current situation. I'm self-employed and have a very lean health insurance plan. Not only they do not cover preventive health such as vaccines (can you believe it?!) but neither do they cover any accidents that occur while abroad or medical emergency evacuations. My goal then was to find travelers medical insurance that would cover any urgent care and transportation back home if needed until I could arrive at the local hospital in my home base for treatment, and then allow my local US health insurance coverage to kick in.

here are many companies that offer traveler medical insurance. I personally like Seven Corners, but there's also World Nomads and Allianz. When you start your research, first, you have to understand what your current regular medical insurance covers while you are abroad. Second, you have to understand what more you need to cover. Third, you have to shop around for what best fits your needs because there are too many choices out there, but keep your goal in mind, which is understanding what you have, what you need, and exactly what to do under all possible scenarios. This means that you should electronically gather serial numbers and receipts of your most expensive equipment should they get lost or stolen. Especially if you are in the process of becoming a digital nomad and your livelihood relies solely on pictures or content uploaded. That expensive camera, GoPro, lenses, laptop, and other peripherals are what puts food on the table so to speak. You should make sure that your trip insurance covers these items. You should also understand the process to follow should you need to replace them so that your downtime is kept at a minimum.

For starters, here's a list of items that you should know if they are covered within your policy and if so, how much. There might be items that are important to you and some that you don't need. Some of these items might already be covered by your current health insurance company that you won't have to add to your travel policy. Whichever insurance agency you choose, make sure you ask a lot of questions and have a full understanding of what you're purchasing:

- o Airline Baggage Claim
- o Doctor's Visit (New Condition)
- o Doctor's Visit (Pre-Condition)
- o Emergency Room
- o Evacuation due to:
  - Global Pandemic
  - Natural Disaster
  - Personal Medical Emergency
  - Political (Terrorism)
- o Hospital Stay
- o Lost or Stolen Equipment
- o Medicine
- o Trip Cancellation
- o Trip Interruption
- o Vaccines

Additionally, here are other basic concepts of the possible coverage points that you should expect to choose from the insurance companies that specialize in travel. At minimum, understand what they are and how to proceed should your insurance policy does not cover it:

Assault

- This rider covers hospitalization, day surgery and out-patient treatment, as well as visits to registered medical practitioners, prescribed medicines, ambulances, and extra expenses to get you home if medically necessary.
- It does not cover assault as a result of picking a fight, since you're putting yourself at risk.
- The laws and customs in some countries are very complex and sometimes victims are imprisoned despite the horrific circumstances. If you are unsure as to what to do, contact your emergency assistance team

immediately, as they will have extensive experience in the matter.

Baggage

- This rider covers damaged baggage while checked-in, stolen baggage, lost baggage while in-transit, stolen passport, prescribed medication.
- It also covers checked-in bags if delayed by at least 12 hours (24 hours in some policies) from the scheduled arrival time. This policy only covers the essentials such as t-shirts, underwear, socks, toiletries, prescribed medication, and other essential items as specified on the policy.

Dental Insurance

- This rider covers an unexpected infection or a broken tooth. It also covers you if you injure your mouth or jaw in an accident.
- It does not cover general check-ups, getting teeth straightened, new teeth or fillings, or major dental work such as crowns, dentures, bridges, or implants.

Health Travel Insurance

- Health travel insurance covers medical emergencies, but it's not designed to cover ongoing illnesses or treatment overseas, or any treatment when you get home.
- Hospitalization, day surgery and out-patient treatment, visits to registered medical practitioners, prescribed medicines, ambulances, extra expenses to get you home if medically necessary
- Some insurance companies will not cover health treatment for diseases that could have been prevented with vaccine.

Medical Repat

- Transportation to get back home: air ambulance, seal level aircraft, helicopter, ground ambulance, flight changes, flight upgrade + medical staff

Natural Disasters

- Natural disasters cannot only cause physical harm, they can also shut down airports and cancel trips. A policy that covers natural disasters will normally cover trip cancellations, trip interruptions, trip delays, medical expenses, baggage loss, 24/7 assistance.
- Natural disaster insurance does not cover you if you don't follow the advice of the authorities, if you hang around to watch what happens, or if you buy a policy after an event becomes known.
- If you are travelling to a region that is known for natural disasters, it's a good idea to do some research to see if there have been any warnings. If you buy a policy after an event is known and the natural disaster impacts your trip, you won't be covered for any expenses.

Pre-Need Insurance

- Return of your remains to your home country, local cremation or burial overseas, reasonable additional expenses for someone to return with your remains.
- Pre-need is not covered if a pre-existing condition causes your death. Pre-need does not cover any costs within your home country once your remains are returned to your next of kin.

Stolen Passport

- While this rider won't cover a pre-trip cancellation or the cost of an emergency passport while traveling, it will at least cover the extra costs while you're delayed and will allow you access to a 24-hour emergency assistance team.

- This rider will not cover costs if the passport is left behind or if you don't take proper precautions to protect your passport, if you don't obtain a written policy to report if it's stolen, or if customs or another government body confiscates your passport for any reason.

Terrorism

- Hospitalization, out-patient treatment, prescribed medicines, medical transportation to come home, flight cancellations + emergency assistance team

Travel Accidents

- Hospitalization, day surgery and out-patient treatment, visits to registered medical practitioners, prescribed medicines, medical evacuation including air ambulance

Trip Cancellation

- A doctor certifies that you're medically unfit to travel; you, your travel buddy, or a close relative is hospitalized or dies

Before you leave:

o Find and scan receipts of the items you're taking with you.
o Take a picture of everything you're taking.
o If an airline loses your gear, report it to them immediately and get it in writing.
o If your items have been stolen, report it to the police within 24 hours. Then file a claim, as they will need a copy of the police report.
o Understand how to block any digital device that could be blocked in case it gets stolen.

As always, be very thorough in your research for both health and travel insurance. Being prepared can be the difference between filling out a form and getting a quick replacement of what you may have lost, and ruining part of your trip or wasting money unnecessarily. Bottom line, know what you're covered for, always read the fine print, and absolutely know what the exclusions are.

NOTE: The information in this section is to the best of my knowledge and intended accurate research, up to date as of the publishing of this revised 1st edition (Corona edition). In fact, when the World Health Organization declared COVID-19 a global pandemic on February 3, 2020, all insurance agencies that offered travel/health insurance had to protect their assets by stipulating that trip cancellations, flight rescheduling, and evacuations due to Coronavirus were not going to be covered by the existing policies as specified under an insurance clause called "Force Majeure" (or act of God). This is a legal term that stipulates that no party is at fault if there is an unforeseeable circumstance that prevents someone from fulfilling a contract. Examples of a force majeure is a pandemic, a war, or a natural disaster. As a result, hundreds of thousands of travelers were left unprepared to figure things out on their own, without the ability to file a claim to evacuate them back home. Now more than ever, you need to understand what your travel policy entails, what it covers and what it doesn't.

TASK 18.1

Make a list of the companies, categories, and items that you want to compare between both your regular health insurance and traveler medical insurance companies. Contact those companies to determine the best fit for you. A few other things to consider: make sure that all of your digital equipment is covered, as well as a medical emergency evacuation. Get a digital copy of your insurance policy, which includes contact info and phone numbers. Share this information with someone close to you and make them your emergency contacts.

STEP 19

Apply for an International Driving Permit

The International Driving Permit is documentation that allows you to legally drive abroad. However, it is not a stand-alone document; in fact, you must present it along with your home-based driver's license. In reality, it just serves as a 'universal' document that backs up your actual driver's license and provides a translation of the different sections of your driver's license in 9 different languages. It is not a government issued ID, so it will not help you identify yourself at the airport or in front of authorities.

If you want to legally drive in another country, you need to obtain an International Driving Permit, but not all countries recognize this document, so be sure to research that piece of information before you apply for it. Keep in mind, however, that this permit is good only for the type license that you already have. For example, in Asia or Europe, riding a scooter is very common, but in order for you to be able to rent one, you must have a motorcycle endorsement on your driver's license. Without that endorsement, you are technically not authorized to ride a scooter or a motorcycle. Same with commercial vehicles. Be sure you get all the necessary endorsements first before applying for your International Driving Permit so as to avoid any inconvenience. Now, I'm sure that someone out there has been able to rent a motorcycle, a scooter, or even a car with just their local license without needing an International Driving Permit. I personally will want to avoid driving in a different country if at all possible; however, in case of an emergency or if I really want to rent a car, I will want the freedom to be able to do so without any hassles.

You can apply for one at the American Automobile Association (better known as AAA) or the American Automobile Touring Alliance (AATA) and the process is fast and easy.

I did find another option, the International Driver's Document, and it's issued by International-License.com. I was very skeptical at the beginning, but I applied for it online anyway. The application process not only is easier than applying for the International Driver's Permit, but the program seems to be more robust. This entity offers an international driver's document for 1, 2, or even 3 years (as opposed to AAA, which is only good for one year). They state that anyone that offers more than 3-year validity is not a legit entity. I actually got my kit in the mail within 48 hours. I was very impressed, and it looks so much more professional than the booklet I got at AAA. Not only did I receive a booklet, but also an ID. Additionally, they have an app that I can access and modify my profile and upload my local driver's license. I can even pick the language I want to translate my driver's license into, which is pretty much what the role of the International Driving Permit is, but much better. It really looks a lot more legit than the one issued by AAA (sorry, AAA, time to up your game). So far, I have not had issues with this documentation when I've presented it.

DRIVER'S LICENSE TRANSLATION

INTERNATIONAL DRIVER'S DOCUMENT

VALID FOR DRIVER'S LICENSE FROM
UNITED STATES

This is a translation of a foreign driving permit in
9 languages by IDL Services Inc.

Image 2: *Driver License Translation – International Driver's Document*

TASK 19.1

Initiate the process to obtain your International Driver's Permit. Whether you have the intention to drive while abroad or not, you want to be able to do so in case a situation requires it.

Sort Bank Accounts and Choose Credit Cards

There are only three instances where you will need to access funds while abroad: on purchases of products and services (i.e., a meal at a restaurant); cash through an ATM machine (i.e., if the local taxi only accepts cash); and virtually, so you can pay bills. Purchases of products and services can be done using either a debit card or a credit card. Call the bank and the credit card companies in advance of your trip to let them know of your travel plans. If they detect unusual activity, they will block your account until they hear back from you. Do not call them from the airport or from any public place where people around you can overhear your personal information. Scan your debit cards and credit cards (back and front), encrypt them and email them to yourself before your trip in case they need to be replaced. Don't forget to add their international collect (or free) phone number to your contacts.

Have a minimum of an ATM card and a couple of credit cards. Ideally, consider one of them as your primary card so if it malfunctions (for example, the magnetic strip gets damaged) or gets 'eaten' by the ATM machine outside of business hours, or it gets hacked and needs to get cancelled, at least you will have a backup plan while waiting for the replacement. Make sure that all of your bank accounts are linked to each other so that you can move money between them if needed. Same with your credit cards, make sure that they are already set up on your bill pay system for both bank accounts. Whichever card you make your primary one is up to you. I chose the one that gives me one mile per dollar spent so I can accumulate enough for a plane ticket.

In terms of ATM cards, I personally try to use Fidelity's My Smart Cash account (Fidelity Visa debit card) when I know that I'll perform a transaction that will get hit with an ATM fee. Fidelity reimburses ATM fees every month and there's not a minimum balance required to maintain the account or to benefit from all of the features of this Visa debit card. The only caveat is that there isn't a physical bank associated with My Smart Cash since Fidelity isn't a bank, but rather an investment company. This means that I cannot physically go to a branch and deposit money. There aren't many limitations (and I've had this card for over 12 years now) but just in case, I have it linked to my other banks' checking accounts, making it easier to transfer funds between accounts. So far, it's been reliable throughout the United States, Europe, Japan, and South America. Bear in mind that Fidelity charges 1% FTF (Foreign

Transaction Fees) on ATM withdrawals and foreign transactions.

Credit Unions are great when it comes to fees. In particular, the State Department Federal Credit Union (SDFCU) Visa credit card charges no annual fee, no FTF and no fees on purchases.

The website www.sdfcu.org/how-do-i-join provides a list of eligible organizational affiliations and states. If you are unable to join through any of the other methods, as a consumer, you may be eligible to join this credit union through the American Consumer Council (ACC), a nonprofit advocacy group. When opening your SDFCU account, you will need to choose 'ACC' on your application. Note that ACC membership "is available to any American consumer who currently uses or has purchased a major consumer product or service…" Their list of categories of products and services includes, "motor vehicle, housing, medical services, financial services, insurance, education, transportation, personal services, apparel, recreation and communications or technology equipment."

One piece of advice: try to identify where the closest ATMs are to where you'll be before you get there. The less you stand out as a tourist, the better, and there is nothing like a non-local asking for directions to an ATM. Avoid that scenario if at all possible. As a side note, if you are trying to withdraw money from an ATM abroad and the transaction gets denied when you specify to withdraw funds from your 'checking account', try selecting 'savings account' instead. I am unsure why, but that usually works.

There is a conglomerate of world banks that have an agreement and don't charge ATM fees if using one of their allies. It's called the Global ATM Alliance, the principal international banking network. Note that Bank of America is the only US bank; however, it charges 3% on currency withdrawals, even for banks within this conglomerate. These are the banks and respective countries belonging to this group:

- ABSA: South Africa
- Bank of America: USA
- Barclays: England, Wales, Spain, Portugal, Gibraltar
- BNP Paribas: France, Ukraine
- China Construction Bank: China
- Deutsche Bank: Germany, Poland, Czech Republic, Spain, Portugal, Italy
- Santander Serfin: Mexico
- Scotiabank: Canada, Peru, Chile, Caribbean, Mexico
- Westpac: Australia, New Zealand, Fiji, Vanuatu, Cook Islands, Samoa, Tonga, Papua New Guinea, Solomon Islands
- UkrSibbank: Ukraine

Wherever you are in the world, you might also be asked if you want your purchase to be processed in USD instead of the local currency. This is known as Dynamic Currency Conversion (DCC). It sounds like it offers a service to customers, but don't be fooled. DCC should always be avoided. When possible, choose to pay in the local currency. Even if it might be simpler to see the costs in dollars, you can be sure that the foreign currency exchange rates applied are pretty poor - meaning you get a worse deal overall. By using DCC, you're basically giving the local company or ATM machine permission to use its own rate to make the conversion on the spot. While your bank wants to keep you happy because you're a valued customer, a foreign provider has no such obligation. They'll see a quick buck, and have no problem marking up the exchange rate and pocketing the difference.

TASK 20.1

Decide which debit and credit cards you'll bring. Call them and tell them about your travel plans. Understand what is needed should one of your cards get lost or stolen and you need to replace them. Make sure that you understand all of the fees involved with all transaction types.

Talk to Your Current Employer (Maybe)

This is definitively a tricky topic. Only you know your employer and can (somewhat) anticipate the way that your manager or company will react to the news of you leaving for a year. There are many aspects to consider: Are they able to hold your position for a year? Could they retaliate by letting you go as soon as you share your plans with them? Are they willing to write a recommendation letter before you depart? Should you let them know months in advance, or only two weeks in advance?

I can offer two perspectives since I worked for 11 years in a large corporation that was centered on employee satisfaction.

Even though there wasn't a formal extended leave of absence program to travel the world, I think I could have worked something out with them. Of course, it would have been unpaid, no doubt, but at least I would have had the security (then again, nothing is guaranteed in this world except for death and taxes) that I could have come back to my job. I'm not a betting woman, but I would have almost bet that I could've advanced in my career even quicker because of that year's exposure to traveling the world. Especially in the area where I was.

Unfortunately, when I decided to travel the world, I was no longer working for this large corporation, but rather, for a very small office. I know that they would have been supportive of me leaving for a year, but I also know that they would not have been able to hold my position for that long. I was in sales for that matter, and for obvious reasons, this company would have had to find a replacement as soon as possible. I know that they wouldn't have let me go right away, but I have the feeling that as soon as my replacement would have been trained, they would've had to waive goodbye, regardless of where I was in my process.

Fortunately, for me, it didn't have to get to that point because I left that job months prior to the start of my travels. In fact, I was a free agent for months, which I utilized to the fullest to be as set up as possible while working on getting monetized before embarking on my journey. In fact, having built a timeline of 365 days put the necessary pressure on me to work extra hard to meet that personal goal. I knew no weekends or holidays. I worked more hours a week than I have ever worked for an employer, and I was known at the financial corporation I worked for 11 years as the biggest workaholic, so that gives you an idea. But I did it with joy, because for the first time, I wasn't making someone else rich; instead, I was working to build my own business and personal brand. How much would you sacrifice during just one year, if you could have everything you ever dreamed of after that?

TASK 21.1

Start researching your company's extended leave of absence policy without disclosing much information, initially. Do not discuss your plans with anybody, unless you have to. Most definitely, do not discuss your plans with anybody from the office, not even your office bestie. Once you're ready to share the news, ask for a letter of recommendation (if that is a possibility) in case they are unable to hold your job as they had promised, or you decide to find another job altogether upon your return.

Book Your Flight!

This is one of the milestones that you've been waiting for a long time. This represents all of the hard work and sweat that you've put into transforming your life. You are finally ready to take a leap of faith and live life on your terms. Or are you? As exciting as this aspect of planning should be, for most of us, it could be overwhelming and a source of anxiety. That is absolutely normal. In fact, after Step 25 and right before the conclusion, I included an on-point article that recommends a healthy way to manage stress as written for this book by a therapist friend, Julie DiNuoscio, and it's titled "Self-Care: Physical and Emotional". For now, let's focus on helping you find the best and cheapest flight available.

Find the cheapest flight through great sites like www.hopper.com, matrix.itasoftware.com, or www.skyscanner.com, but then buy directly from the airline. These sites will compare various flights from multiple companies to help you find the cheapest options. You can typically search by specific dates, or just the cheapest month, so you can get an overall view of pricing, which can be helpful if you have flexible dates. But when you identify the flight that best suits your needs, you want to go straight to that airline's website and buy it directly from them. The reason for this is because if the flight gets cancelled, agents at the airport will be able to make a change for you on the spot or at least refer you to their customer service, who will be able to work faster on the issue, but only if you purchased the ticket directly from that website. On the other hand, they will be more limited in the changes that they might be able to make if you purchased the ticket through a third-party site, such as Priceline or Orbit. I worked for two years for the largest airline in the US and it was very frustrating for both the passengers and the airline employees to have to refer customers to the website where they bought the ticket from if any changes needed to be made.

It will also be beneficial for you to enroll in as many loyalty programs as possible through airlines in order to get mileage and awards. This will help you in the long run to save money on flights in the future. For example, I have travelled to Chile and to Japan for free with those miles and next year I will be able to go to Australia for free.

Depending on the type of trip that you have planned, you could buy your tickets as you decide where to go next or you can buy your tickets in advance. One option gives you more flexibility than the other, but at the same time, buying all of your airfare in advance might save you money in the long run, even though it requires much more planning upfront. An alternative to consider is to purchase a 'Round The World' ticket, also known in airline jargon as an RTW. These tickets are intended to allow you to travel to multiple places at a discounted price and they are airline alliance flight passes. An airline alliance is a partnership in which airlines share seats on planes, passengers, and elite status benefits. You buy a ticket from one airline that can be used with them and their partners for one price, which lets you travel around the world on that one ticket.

There are several companies that offer this option, though you won't be able to utilize some of the more "budget friendly" airlines that certain countries have (i.e. Frontier or SouthWest). However, this does allow you the option to travel to multiple cities within various countries, based on the number of miles you purchase. Most RTW tickets offer bundles based on miles (i.e. 29,000, 34,000, etc.) and will get you a certain number of stops. There are very specific rules affiliated with these types of tickets, so be sure to do a lot of research beforehand. Here are the three main alliances. Look for the 'Round The World' or RTW section within each:

- OneWorld Alliance www.oneworld.com
- Star Alliance at www.startalliance.com
- SkyTeam Alliance at www.skyteam.com

While it is notoriously difficult to get an upgrade on airline seats these days (the process is typically automated electronically), it never hurts to ask. You can ask during check-in or ask the gate attendant if it would be possible to get an upgrade. It's good to dress professionally and be polite (as they deal with many cranky customers on a regular basis) to try and increase your chances. Be aware that typically, the person with the highest-ranking flight status, the person who paid for a seat that's eligible for upgrade, or the person who used their miles, are most likely to get it. However, there's never any harm in asking, and you might find yourself in a slightly cozier seat as a result!

Now more than ever, airlines are skimming on meals and most everything at the airport is much more expensive. Therefore, for the sake of saving money, I strongly recommend that you (1) head to the airport with a full belly, and (2) if at all possible, bring snacks or an already prepared sandwich, or anything that you think will hold you over until the next warm meal so you don't have to spend unnecessarily at the airport. The exception for this is drinks, since you can't go through security with liquids over 3oz. However, you can get in the habit of carrying an empty water bottle, since most airports have filtered water fountains. This is a good way to be economic and save extra money for more important items on your trip.

Lastly, here's an interesting website that allows you to view ratings for airlines, airports, and lounges. There's nothing like being unprepared for having a five-hour layover in a tiny airport with little food/entertainment options. You can check all that out at www.skytraxratings.com to get a sense of what to expect during your airline travels.

TASK 22.1

Enroll in all the reward programs that you can and ensure that each of these airlines' profiles have the necessary information along with your passport number and Global Entry number, if applicable. Keep a file with all of your frequent flyer information, which includes all your airlines' and hotels' loyalty info.

STEP 23

Select Phone Plans or Mi-Fi's

Generally speaking, there are five options when it comes to cell phone communication overseas.

(1) You can keep your current carrier, but upgrade to a plan that will allow you to make calls internationally. Through my carrier, which claims to be the best one in the US, I find this option a little bit expensive because I have had to pay $10 a day to have phone and data access when traveling internationally. I understand that other carriers' international plans are much more economical, but the quality of service might be on the line, no pun intended. Do your research thoroughly so that there are no surprises. The benefit of

keeping your carrier while you travel abroad, whether you pay for their international plan or not, is that you get to keep your phone number.

(2) You can get a local SIM card from each country that you visit and pay as you go. If this is what you choose to do, before you leave, make sure that you contact your carrier and confirm that your phone is unlocked. Make sure you keep your carrier's SIM card in a safe place for when you get back, otherwise, your phone won't work. Know that if you lose it, you can buy a new one directly from your carrier for about $25. Getting local SIM cards is probably the cheapest option; each country will have many plans, so make sure you chose the right one for you. I got a really good deal last year in Spain for a $25-dollar SIM card which gave me 25GB and 150 local minutes. Connection is usually very good. If you buy a SIM card in an EU country, it should work in all EU countries - same in the Caribbean. The downfall, however, is that you don't get to keep your phone number while using the local SIM card. However, if you are like me and use WhatsApp to connect with friends and family, when you use it for the first time under the new SIM card it will ask you whether you want to maintain your original number or want to switch to the local number. This is totally your choice, but I always keep my original number. You can also use Facebook Messenger if you need to communicate with people back at home who are not on WhatsApp. The app Line is also a great alternative. Also, remember that you can buy a local prepaid phone in the country you'll be going to specifically, but price comparison might only be advantageous if you stay in that specific country for over 6 months.

(3) You could also buy a global SIM card at Flexiroam.com. I personally have not tried this. I looked into it and compared plans and felt that it was very expensive. In this category, I'll include Google Fi. In fact, Google Fi seems to be the best option, based on all of the reviews, and is the most economical of the global SIM cards out there. An unlimited international plan could be about $70 a month, which is very good. Otherwise, a regular eSIM card might not be the cheapest option compared to buying local SIM cards, but at least you don't have to mess with switching SIM cards every time you arrive in a different country. For instance, with Flexiroam, I can get 11GB of data which I can use within a year anywhere for $325 dollars. But what do I do with 11GB? Not a whole lot. I found other options at Amazon, just take a look under the search term "World SIM Card".

(4) Buying a local phone is an option, but won't likely be the most economical alternative, unless you're staying in one place for a long period of time. Just like phone carriers in your area, be mindful of contracts and always choose prepaid options to avoid long-term commitments with that country's phone carrier.

(5) Buy a Mi-Fi, or portable HotSpot where you can connect to Wi-Fi anytime, anywhere. There are way too many options out there - research thoroughly to understand which one is the best choice for your needs by using the term "Portable HotSpots for Travel". Right off the bat, I can tell you that the two major benefits are not having to deal with local SIM cards, and all of the flexibility and autonomy that a portable HotSpot can give you. The downfall is that this is another device that you have to carry with you, although they are not heavy at all. They are probably the priciest option if you take into

consideration not just the hardware itself but the data plans that you have to keep reloading. I rented one when I went to Japan and it was very useful, but I only needed it for a month, so it was very affordable.

Here is a very rudimentary comparison table of options based on how long you'll be gone and the number of countries that you will be visiting. This is not a scientific study, so please just take it for what it is. I created it because when I went backpacking for a year to 12 different countries and needed to see what my best option was, I made a chart to compare all of my options and prices and this was the end result:

Phone Plans and Connection Options

LENGTH OF STAY AND NUMBER OF COUNTRIES	**1** KEEP CURRENT CARRIER	**2** * LOCAL SIM CARD	**3** * GLOBAL SIM CARD	**4** LOCAL PHONE	**5** PORTABLE HOT STPOT (MI-FI)
1 Week to 1 Month 1 - 2 countries	$-$$$	$	varies	$$$$	$$
1 week to 1 month 3+ countries	$-$$$	$	varies	$$$$	$$
1 month to 6 months 1 - 3 countries	$-$$$	$	varies	$$$	$$$$
1 month to 6 months 4+ countries	$-$$$	$$	varies	$$$$	$$$$
6 months to +1 year 1 - 4 countries	$$$$$	$$	$$$$$	$$-$$$$	$$$$
6 months to +1 year 5+ countries	$$$$$	$$$	$$$$$	$$$$	$$$$

2 * Some local SIM cards will work in contiguos countries, usually between European and the Caribbean countries.

3 * There are too many options for global SIM cards, beware of phone and OS requirements.

Table 15

Right before starting my year off, my plan was going to be to suspended service with my phone and pay $10 a month to keep my number and just buy local SIM cards. I almost went with Google Fi, but I couldn't because I have an Apple phone and Apple phones purchased through my specific US carrier were not compatible with Google Fi at that moment. I quote directly from their website, "[Google Fi] is currently in BETA on iPhones and currently there is no network switching capability". So, no Google Fi for me just yet. Things might be different in a year, in a different continent, who knows. But for folks looking to do the nomad thing like I am, I want to share the following hack with you: get one of those stainless-steel credit card holders from Amazon for about $10. This is where I put all my SIM cards and write down the local phone number on them along with the purchase date. If I go back to that country, I just recharge it and reuse it, and this is usually cheaper than getting a brand new one.

TASK 23.1

There are so many choices when it comes to staying connected and keeping up with your line of work while monetizing abroad. The cost of staying connected and being able to do your job remotely will depend on whether you're going to more than one country and the length of each stay. Research all of your options and always choose what's best for you, even if that costs a little bit more.

Decide if Storage is Needed

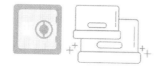

Having lived in the US for over 28 years, I can attest to the cultural perspective that collecting material possessions is seemingly a standard of success. I'm neither rallying for it nor condemning it. In fact, I'm not passing any sort of judgement or generalizing thinking that everyone in this country goes by those standards. This is just an objective observation that we, as a culture, have a tendency to accumulate more things than any other culture combined. Sure, economics may play a big part in it, given the higher purchasing power that we have compared to other countries. More importantly, I'm not excluding myself in these statistics because when I started my minimalistic life for the sake of planning my gap year, I realized how much useless crap I had accumulated since I had moved to the United States. That realization was pretty humbling at best and embarrassing at worst, yet it was a great opportunity to look within to understand how and why I got to be a hoarder. The answers may fill a whole book, but for the purpose of providing you with my best perspective on the topic to help you travel the world more efficiently, all I'm going to say is: Get rid of the most you can!

At this point, and as we discussed in Step 12, the book Essentials: Essays of the Minimalists by Joshua Fields Millburn and Ryan Nicodemus inspired me to get rid of most everything I owned. I was able to sell, donate, and give away most of it and it felt really good. I was able to leave as-is things like furniture and appliances since I wanted to rent out my house completely furnished. Since I was only taking a 50-liter backpack, I could only fit a very few personal belongings, especially since half of the backpack contained all of my electronics to maintain content for my blog, YouTube channel, website, and any possible freelance work I could land on to support myself while traveling. In fact, most of the items in my backpack are my laptop, mirrorless camera, GoPro, tripod, studio headphones, rechargeable batteries, slim hard drive, power battery bank, all kinds of cables and wires, outlet adaptors, and all those sorts of things. This means that there was still a lot that I had to leave behind.

Whether you have a house to come back to or you don't, leaving things behind could be a very difficult thing to do. I went through all of the things I thought I was leaving behind and storing about 10 times, and each time I was able to throw away a few more items. But there were still things that I could not part with such as my precious hybrid bike or my favorite painting called, 'The Singing Butler' by Scottish painter Jack Vettriano (not the original painting, of course, but still) which beautifully displayed over my eggplant-colored living room walls. Part of this list of items that I could not ever get rid of was a collection of the books I grew up reading that reminded me of my childhood years in Chile, and the collection of cookbooks from all of the countries I had visited up until that point. What was I supposed to do? If you are able to get rid of everything, hats off to you. But if you, like myself, are still emotionally tied to things that are irreplaceable or are planning on coming back to home base, then storage might be the only solution. I purposely opted for the smallest storage unit available so that I couldn't store much. It's a 5 x 5 and I pay about $20 a month.

When shopping for a storage facility, I looked at several things. First, location was important for me because I didn't want to drive too far when making trips as I was moving items into it. I started renting two months prior to my departure date because I wanted to start moving items a little bit at a time and I was able to get the first month for free just to try it out. Another factor was, of course, size and pricing. The bigger the storage room, the more expensive it was going to be. Limiting the space forced me to downsize even more. A third factor was their security system. The storage facility I chose not only had a gate that could only be opened by an electronic key, but also had surveillance cameras recording 24/7. Not like I had anything of high value, but I didn't want to deal with vandalism or anything like that either.

But if you do have to rent a full-size room because you have to leave furniture and much more behind, be sure to ask a friend or someone you trust to check on your things once a month or so. The most important aspect is to ensure that there is no sign of forced entry through the rolling door (or any type of door) to your storage room. Keep payments automated in case you come back later than anticipated and always keep the business owner's information in case of an emergency.

TASK 24.1

Start assessing the size of the storage room that you might need and seriously consider doing without one. If you have to have one, start shopping around and create a chart of pros and cons of each so that you can make the best decision on which storage facility you should choose.

STEP 25

Arrange for Mail Delivery Options

This last step was proven to be by far the most challenging for me. I own a house in my home base of Cincinnati, Ohio, which I'll be renting out. I have no family members living locally who I can ask to check on my mail or that I can forward my mail to. I cannot forward my mail to the post office because I can't ask anybody to collect it on a weekly basis. There are companies out there that can manage mail for you, but they are insanely expensive. I have many friends, but I don't want to burden anyone by forwarding them my mail. The best solution I found, though not optimal, was to install a second mailbox next to the first one just for my mail and have a friend collect the mail only on a monthly basis, hoping for the best.

If you are able to forward your mail to someone else, that's certainly going to be the best and most economical option. You simply change your address at the post office online at www.usps.com and your problem is solved. In order to help everybody involved, start by contacting all of the companies that you can and switch to electronic billing. Ensure that you are able to log onto their accounts online and keep track of your customer IDs.

Your next step should be to unsubscribe from snail mail, it's almost like a 'Do Not Call' list for junk mail. It's as simple as going to www.DMAChoice.org, which is a tool offered by the Data & Marketing Association that lets you remove your name and address from a number of these lists for only $2. You can also unsubscribe from those preapproved credit cards and insurance offers by going to www.OptOutPrescreen.com a service offered by major credit bureaus.

If these options don't work for you, you could look into getting a virtual mailbox, but that could be insanely expensive depending on the type of plan that you select. The prices for these services range greatly, depending on whether you're an individual, a business, and what type of perks you're looking for from the company. A virtual mailbox company will get you set up with a physical mailing address and they will manage your mail for you. Physical addresses are typically better than a P.O. Box, since some government and financial institutions won't mail to a P.O. Box. A list of the services that you can choose from are:

- Forwarding (to wherever you are at the moment)
- Online Storage (unlimited)
- Open & Scan (so you can view the piece of mail and take action if needed)

- Physical Storage (normally free for 30 days but then charged per item per day)
- Shredding

The most popular and prestigious company that I know is called Any Time Mailbox and their website is www.anytimemaibox.com. I think that they are a great alternative for people like myself who have no family in town to help with mail forwarding options. Unfortunately, at the moment, their prices are prohibitive to someone without a steady income, but if you can afford it, then by all means check it out or any other virtual mailbox alternatives out there. It's worth noting that check deposit and recycling are not available services yet with this company.

Related to virtual mailboxes and as a side note, since it's a federal offense for someone to open your mail without your consent, you'll want to fill out a USPS Form 1083 and have it notarized, giving the third party the authorization to handle your mail. You can do this either in person at a post office or use an online notary (fees usually start around $25). After that, you should be all set to have your mail managed by any of these virtual companies, or by a friend. Bon voyage!

TASK 25.1

Assess your mailing options depending on whether you are coming back to your home base and if you have friends and family members that you can rely on to help you with this task. Unsubscribe to the most mailers you can and switch to electronic billing and bill automation when possible.

Physical and Emotional

By Julie DiNuoscio

While in the process of discovering your passions, you are going to want to discern how to take care of your personal well-being. You can love what you do, but if you're getting burned out by not attending to your personal needs, it can be easy to lose sight of the overall goal. Sometimes we can love something so much that we dedicate almost too much time or energy to it and forget to slow down and check in with ourselves and rest as needed. Our goal here is to help you think through what you can be putting in place for yourself to ensure you're continuing to be well while traveling and doing what you love.

When preparing for a trip, it's essential to first prepare yourself, both physically and emotionally, for your time away. Consider how much you'll be walking. Most countries have public transportation, and if you're planning on backpacking, you'll likely be walking or using public transit more than driving around places. Therefore, figure out an exercise regimen that works for you to build up some endurance. Especially work on cardio and building up leg strength. You don't want to find yourself completely worn out after only a few miles. Practice your cardio with your packed backpack on and work on building muscle strength in your shoulders/back to prepare your body for the new way you'll be carrying yourself.

I'd also recommend incorporating daily stretching into your routine. You can do this simply with a YouTube or exercise video, by taking a yoga class, or by doing all of those fun stretches you learned in gym class! Stretching is a great way to speed up muscle recovery and prevent injuries, which will be important after walking/hiking for hours at a time.

As far as self-care goes emotionally, take some time to process and prepare yourself before you travel. Consider what your emotional needs are and how you plan to get them met in another environment. How do you plan to stay connected to others at home? What will you do when you're feeling lonely? If you're in a panic because something went wrong (missed a plane/bus, lost your passport, etc.) are you aware of ways to calm yourself down so that you can think clearly and get things taken care of? Practice mindfulness before you leave. This will tremendously help with your emotion regulation while you're away. Mindfulness is essentially exercising the "coming back to present" muscle. Therefore, don't worry about emptying your mind; instead, focus on coming back to the present moment. If your mind starts to wander, no worries – let the thoughts float away from you and come back to the present moment (you could do this by focusing on your breath). Some people practice mindfulness when washing their hands or brushing their teeth (since it's something they do more than once a day). This is done by focusing on the temperature, texture, and pressure that you're noticing. What colors and smells are you aware of? Focusing on this will flex that muscle of staying in the present moment. If you're having a hard time with that, use the 5, 4, 3, 2, 1 method: what are 5 things you see, 4 things you physically feel (cold wind, hard book in your hands, etc.), 3 things you hear, 2 things you smell, and 1 thing you taste. Your mind physically cannot think two things at once, so if you are focusing on what you're experiencing in the present moment, that gives your body time to calm down so you can tackle the current worry or problem that you are dealing with.

If you are a writer, consider bringing a journal along to give yourself space to process your time away. Culture shock alone will stir up a lot internally, so it can be nice to let the feelings/experiences flow on paper. If you're more of a verbal processor, consider keeping a video diary of your experiences so that you can talk out what you've been going through. If you draw, get some paper and pastels wherever you go and express yourself that way. No matter how you process, figure out a way to continue to do so while you're traveling. It is incredibly valuable to your mental health to be able to take some time to decompress and move through your feelings, rather than shoving them down and ignoring them until stress hits and they all come tumbling out.

By maintaining both physical and emotional self-care, you'll be able to carry yourself well throughout your travels. Of course, there will be moments of tiredness, loneliness, confusion, etc. but having a plan in advance will allow you to combat those challenges faster than if you had no plan. Don't underestimate the importance of that physical and emotional prep-work. Give yourself time to put those practices into place just like you would learning a new language, planning for a trip, or any other activities related to this adventure you're embarking upon. You'll be glad you did!

CONCLUSION

As I finish writing this book, I retrospectively think about all of the lessons I've learned in my 28 years in the United States. I learned to learn, observe, adapt, go with the flow, absorb, be resourceful, be flexible, and to apply myself. I learned to comply with other people's rules, because it was what was needed at the moment. I am finally freeing myself once again and letting myself be the rebel I've always been at heart. As long as I don't harm anyone and love my fellow human beings, I'd say I'm allowed. I remember when I decided to come to the States in 1992 against my mother's wishes. I'll never forget walking around the Tampa airport, the first stopover in the States on my way to college as an exchange student at the State University of Plattsburgh in upstate New York. It was the best feeling ever, even though I couldn't speak a word of English and I had less than $500 in my name. Make that $490 after indulging in 6 tacos from Taco Bell at the airport. I had never had tacos before in my life and I couldn't get enough of them! My mom didn't support my decision to leave home and, therefore, I couldn't count with her financial assistance. I was on my own for the first time in my life, not knowing the language or the way things worked. But somehow, I made it and earned a Psychology degree in 3 years and graduated Cum Laude.

I also remember when I moved from upstate New York to Athens, Ohio in 1995 to go to Ohio University because I had just been offered a full scholarship to complete a master's degree. I had $65 in my pocket and drove a 1982 navy blue Ford LTD. I slept in my car for the first two weeks after I arrived to this small college town in the Midwest because I couldn't afford an apartment like the other college kids. But I didn't care because I knew that I was going to figure things out. And I did. I graduated with honors 2 years later and my career blossomed after that. My point in sharing all of this is, I have never been scared to follow my heart, even if things were less than optimal. Just like a lot of people, who I call my tribe, I have an adventurous spirit. Not everybody can understand that, but if you are reading this book right now and putting things into practice, I have a feeling that you do. You have my utmost respect and I wish you the best on your own adventures.

I stand here not knowing how things are going to work out during my first year as a world nomad, but one thing I know for a fact: things will work out somehow. Only in two instances have I worked as hard as I have in this past year, but never for this long though. For the freedom I'm experiencing right now, I would do it all over again if I had to. I cannot wait to hear your own stories of courage and bravery.

May you find what you're looking for,

Maggie

POST SCRIPTUM TO FIRST EDITION

As fate would have it, the COVID-19 pandemic closed all borders just a few days prior to hopping on that plane heading to my first year-long adventure. My entire team and I debated long and hard about whether we should move forward with the publishing of this book or not. At the end, I decided to launch for three reasons.

First, the fact that I couldn't travel did not tarnish the integrity of the content. The book is about the steps I took leading to getting on that plane in terms of the practical as well as the financial planification of a gap year. Both these aspects were completed successfully prior to commencing the trip.

Second, even though the confirmed volunteer gigs I had lined up through Work Away and World Packers were consequently cancelled due to COVID-19, this did not change the fact that these are legit ways to travel if you are on a tight budget. Illustrating this aspect was the main objective of the book and that was successfully accomplished despite having to postpone my volunteer work. In no way, shape, or form I have described an event that I did not experience.

And third, it is my personal -and very strong- conviction that my readers would benefit much more from putting the steps outlined in this book into practice now, during the mandated Coronavirus quarantine. I do not believe that there is a better time than now for self-reflection, for starting a minimalist life, and for putting one's financials in order, which are the three pillars of my message all throughout the book. The digital shop I created is up and running and starting to produce; certainly not as much as I had hoped, but it's only expected given the events happening in the world today.

Because of these three reasons, I am moving forward with the publishing this book even though the COVID-19 pandemic has restricted all non-essential travel until further notice. I cannot wait to share with you how everything turns out.

Best regards,

maggie m. gomez

AUTHOR

Cincinnati, Ohio USA, April 1, 2020

Printed in Great Britain
by Amazon